7.95

W9-DIN-523

DISCOVERING
ARCHAEOLOGY

Cover picture: These stones at Callanish in the Hebrides, off the west coast of Scotland, were erected about 1500 BC. In the center of the group, archaeologists have discovered the remains of a grave.

Opposite: A Celtic brooch dating from 6–7 AD. It is made of gold, glass, enamel and semi-precious stones.

DISCOVERING
ARCHAEOLOGY
by Iris Barry

Published by

STONEHENGE

in association with

The American Museum of Natural History

The author
Iris Barry is a working archaeologist at present researching the prehistory of Ecuador. She has an honors degree in Archaeology and Anthropology from the University of Cambridge, and was awarded the Eileen and Phyllis Gibbs Travelling Fellowship from Newnham College, Cambridge for 1978–9. She is the author of a number of books and is a regular contributor to learned journals.

The consultant
Dr Warwick Bray is Reader in Latin American Archaeology at the University of London. He is Vice President of the Royal Anthropological Institute and a Fellow of the Society of Antiquaries. He does excavations in the field every summer, usually in South America, the area which is his specialty. He is a regular and notable contributor to archaeological journals, and has also written a number of books.

The American Museum of Natural History
Stonehenge Press wishes to extend particular thanks to the following officials and staff of The American Museum of Natural History for their counsel and assistance in creating this volume: Dr. Thomas D. Nicholson, Director; Mr. David D. Ryus, Vice-President; Dr. Walter A. Fairservis Junior; Dr Craig Morris and Dr. Enid Schildkrout.

Stonehenge Press Inc.:
Publisher: John Canova
Editor: Ezra Bowen
Deputy Editor: Carolyn Tasker

Trewin Copplestone Books Ltd.:
Editorial Director: James Clark
Managing Editor: Barbara Horn
Executive Editor: Penny Clarke

Created, designed and produced by
Trewin Copplestone Books Ltd, London.

© Trewin Copplestone Books Ltd, 1981

Library of Congress catalogue card number 81-51992
Printed in U.S.A. by Rand McNally & Co.
First printing
ISBN 0-86706-004-2

Set in Monophoto Rockwell Light by
SX Composing Ltd, Rayleigh, Essex, England
Separation by Positive Colour Ltd, Maldon, Essex, England
Printed in U.S.A. by Rand McNally & Co.

Contents

The World of Archaeology	5
The First Archaeologists	6
Discovering Early Civilizations	8
Archaeology from the Air	10
Prospecting for the Past	12
Excavation: 1	14
Excavation: 2	16
Preserving Our Past	18
Remains from the Earth	20
Clues from Plants	22
Digging up Bones	24
The Carbon 14 Revolution	26
Tree-ring Dating	28
Other Dating Methods	30
Fakes and Frauds	32
Historical Archaeology	34
Economic Archaeology	36
Archaeology Underwater	38
Industrial Archaeology	40
Rescue Archaeology	42
Experiments in Archaeology	44
The Origins of Mankind	46
The First Toolmakers	48
Hunters and Gatherers	50
The First Farmers	52
The Origins of Cities	54
Writing and Its Decoding	56
Pottery and the Wheel	58
The Copper Age	60
The Bronze Age	62
The Iron Age	64
Transport by Land and Sea	66
Evidence from Coins	68
Weapons and War	70
Gods and Religion	72
Graves and Tombs	74
Home Life	76
Models, Toys and Games	78
Recreating the Past	80
The Story in Pictures	82
Treasure Hunters	84
Gold and Goldsmiths	86
Myths, Legends and Reality	88
Archaeology and Cultural Anthropology	90
Archaeology Tomorrow	92
Glossary	94
Index and Credits	96

The World of Archaeology

Archaeology is concerned with the fascinating discoveries that have been made and the incredibly detailed information that can be deduced from the remains left behind by our long-vanished ancestors.

Archaeologists work all over the world, in deserts and in tropical rain forests, in the Arctic tundra and in swamps. They are even excavating among the foundations of office buildings in modern cities and in advance of bulldozers digging up new roads. But what are archaeologists really trying to do? Many people think that the purpose of all this digging is to find buried treasure, or at the very least to find yet more ancient pots and unexciting stone tools to join other such objects on dusty museum shelves. But archaeology involves far more than just finding old objects in the ground. Archaeologists work with teams of scientific specialists and a battery of up to date equipment in order to understand and reconstruct precisely how people lived in the past. They want to know how we became so different from our ape-like ancestors millions of years ago, where and when we first started to cultivate the crops and domesticate the animals which now provide our food. Archaeologists examine the distant roots of mankind's history in order to trace the origins and development of our modern world.

Huge monuments, such as Stonehenge in Wiltshire, England and the Serpent Mound in Ohio, have long mystified men and women who were curious to know who built these great structures, and why and when. Archaeology can give near-complete answers to these questions, and often reveals the kernel of truth concealed within folk-tales and legends. King Arthur, for example, cannot be proved to have existed as a person, but excavation of a Dark Age fortress at South Cadbury in Dorset, has given us proof of a powerful chiefdom or court located on one of the traditional sites of Camelot, from which British warriors fought the invading Anglo-Saxons.

Archaeologists work on smaller sites too, and draw their conclusions from what seems the slenderest evidence. Indeed, many of their finds can only be seen under a microscope! In Papua-New Guinea excavations in the Kuk region have produced almost nothing in the way of stone tools, bones, or house remains. Archaeologists working on this site have concentrated on recovering environmental evidence: seeds and pollen trapped in layers of soil, and on patterns of ancient drainage canals and bumps and hollows in the old land surface. They have also collected carbon samples to date their finds by carbon 14 and so discover when farmers first began to plant their crops and settle in this part of the island. To their astonishment the results of many months' hard work in the field and in the laboratory indicated that farmers had been preparing special raised garden plots as long ago as 9000 years and cultivating taro (an important tropical root crop) at least 7000 years ago. These dates have revolutionized theories about the origins and spread of agriculture throughout Southeast Asia.

Discoveries are still being made, whether of great earthworks on the eastern slope of a volcano in the Andes, or a fragment of a fossilized bone from an ancestor of early man in Africa, or even of those tell-tale minute pollen grains. Archaeology is an exciting, changing science and this book will introduce you to it.

The First Archaeologists

People have always marveled at ruins from the past, explaining them away as the works of gods or giants. It was in the mid-fifteenth century that interest in the study of antiquity arose. By the sixteenth and seventeenth centuries, scholars in Europe had begun to take the examination and recording of these remains seriously and to theorize about them. When the Americas and Africa were being explored, Europeans came into contact with unfamiliar peoples and ways of life which they believed could only be explained by looking at the past.

The early archaeologists, or antiquarians as they called themselves, had no way of dating most of the ruins they studied, as there were no written records. They looked for their explanations in the literature and learning of the classical world of the ancient Greeks and Romans, and in the story of the Creation in the Old Testament. However, knowledge of the past grew steadily during the seventeenth and eighteenth centuries when excavations began to be carried out. Digging for treasure in barrows and other burial mounds became a hobby for the educated classes. Stone implements dug from the ground were recognized as the tools of our early ancestors, very like those used by native peoples in the Americas or Africa. Some of these tools were found in the same layers of soil as the bones of extinct mammals.

Unfortunately, the study of the distant past was hindered by the accepted view that the world had been created in 4004 BC. Scholars did not know how literally to take the Biblical accounts of the early history of the world, or how to fit the increasing number of archaeological remains they knew about into such a short span of time. Also, they could not say how old the remains were, unless they contained datable inscriptions or coins.

During the eighteenth century, scientists began to study geology and examine the fossil remains which were found in some rocks. Many realized that the strata of the earth, the layers of different sorts of rocks and soils, showed the order in which these had been laid down. By studying stratification they might reveal the history of the earth. But how could they explain the finds of the fossilized bones of extinct creatures? It was becoming much more difficult to believe that the earth was just a few thousand years old!

By the end of the eighteenth century, excavation techniques were becoming more advanced, and excavators were seriously looking for evidence which would throw light on our past. When C.J. Thomsen tried to organize the national museum col-

During the nineteenth century, many ancient burial mounds were excavated by antiquarians and archaeologists. This idealized view of a team excavating in Louisiana formed part of a panorama of the history of the Mississippi River painted in 1850.

The Aztecs of Mexico decorated this human skull with turquoise mosaic. Their craftsmanship astounded sixteenth-century artists and scholars in Europe.

lection of Denmark, he suggested that all artifacts, things made by human beings, recovered from the ground could be arranged by the three materials used successively, and related to one of three ''Ages'': the Stone, Bronze, and Iron Ages. Now finds could be placed in order and linked to particular types of societies, that is communities of people sharing the same economy, technology and social organization.

In England, early in the nineteenth century, geologists like Sir Charles Lyell argued that the world had been formed and was still forming by slow, gradual processes. The earth was very old and life had existed on it for millions of years. In France, Boucher de Perthes found stone tools together with the bones of extinct animals in the gravel beds of the Somme. He published these discoveries as further evidence of the great antiquity of the human race. The public would not accept these amazing views.

Charles Darwin's theories also met with fierce opposition. He combined all the evidence collected so far with his own observations of living creatures. He suggested that new species evolved by the survival of those best adapted to their environment, and that the human species also had developed and evolved in this way. This seemed to suggest that God was not directly involved in the process of Creation. During the latter part of the nineteenth century these ideas gained ground and the study of archaeology grew fast.

One of the many excavations General Pitt Rivers organized in Dorset, England. He invented many of the methods of excavation still used by archaeologists. His military training showed in the orderly way in which he ran his digs and clearly marked everything of significance found.

Discovering Early Civilizations

While other archaeologists were slowly proving that people had existed for many hundreds of thousands of years before they had started to live in cities governed by priests and kings, a few pioneer archaeologists were uncovering the riches left behind by the earliest civilizations. In the ancient cities scribes kept records which have become our first historical documents, leaving us fascinating details of their history and mythology. Archaeologists of the nineteenth and early twentieth centuries rediscovered civilizations. They revealed great cities and magnificent treasures which stirred the imagination of the world.

One of the first of these discoveries to capture the public's attention was Austen Henry Layard. In the 1840s he worked at Nimrud and Nineveh in Mesopotamia (part of modern Iraq). Both cities are mentioned

Gold mask from a grave at Mycenae. The German archaeologist Heinrich Schliemann believed it portrayed King Agamemnon.

in the Bible although Nimrud was then called Calah. At both sites he made important discoveries. At Nineveh, he unearthed vast palaces and the great library of the Assyrian kings who ruled during the sixth and seventh centuries BC. The library was made up of over 25,000 clay tablets inscribed with cuneiform, or wedge-shaped, writing. Some told stories of

The most important centers of ancient civilizations date from about 3000 BC to 1500 AD. The earliest civilizations probably developed in Mesopotamia and in the Nile valley. The Indus and Shang civilizations followed a little later. In the Americas the first cities were being built from about 500 BC.

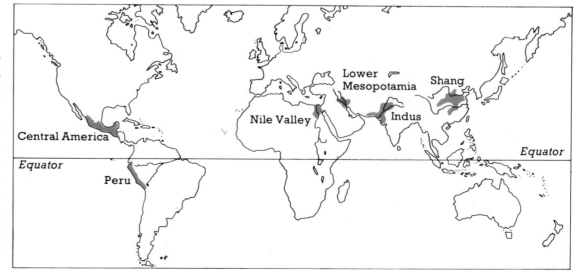

High in the Andes mountains of Peru, the abandoned Inca citadel of Machu Picchu lay forgotten for nearly 400 years, until it was rediscovered by Hiram Bingham, the American explorer and historian who later became a statesman.

gods and heroes. Others revealed details of plant life, herbal cures for many illnesses, and observations of the stars. Layard's discoveries received enormous publicity. With great difficulty he transported some of his most impressive discoveries to London, such as the huge human-headed stone lions and bulls from Nimrud. This whetted the public's appetite.

The next great discovery was made by a retired German trader and banker, Heinrich Schliemann, who began excavating in 1870 on the west coast of Turkey. Schliemann had long believed that the Greek poet Homer's description of the wars between Greeks and Trojans in the *Iliad* and the *Odyssey* was based on a true story. The Greeks besieged the city of Troy because Paris, son of King Priam, had stolen Helen, the beautiful wife of a Greek king. In a few seasons' work, Schliemann was able to prove that Troy lay hidden beneath the mound at Hissarlik, and that he had found the city of King Priam. Schliemann also used Homer to explain what he found. When he discovered a great hoard of golden jewelry, he believed he had found the treasure of the slain King Priam. In 1876 he dug at Mycenae, legendary home of the Greek warrior-king, Agamemnon, who had fought against the Trojans. Schliemann and his team found six graves containing the funeral treasure of a royal family. He claimed that one piece, a mask, showed the face of Agamemnon himself. Many of Schliemann's conclusions and dates are now known

to be wrong. There had been several cities of Troy, each built upon the ruins of the last, and he had dug too deep. But his work has been valuable to archaeologists, for it revealed a civilization that nobody believed had existed.

The task of excavating Knossos on Crete fell to the British archaeologist, Arthur Evans. This was the site of the Labyrinth, or maze, where legend told of youths and maidens sacrificed to a monster – half man, half bull – the Minotaur. Starting in 1899 Evans revealed the remains of a vast and complex palace, which he interpreted as the palace of King Minos, whose wife was mother of the Minotaur. Its many wall-paintings of youths and girls vaulting over the horns of charging bulls were evidence of both the legend and the society from which it sprang.

Amazing discoveries were also being made in the Americas. Explorers identified long-forgotten cities and ceremonial centers. Hiram Bingham climbed the Andes of Peru, in 1911, to discover the "lost city of the Incas," Machu Picchu. The dense jungles of Central America were penetrated, and the first pictures drawn of the ruins of the most fascinating of these ancient civilizations, the Maya. Inscriptions have been found which reveal their advanced knowledge of mathematics and astronomy. But the ruins of huge stone pyramids and scattered cities are all that remain of this great civilization which disappeared over a thousand years ago.

Archaeology from the Air

During World War I, photographs of the ground were taken from aircraft for military purposes. By accident it was noticed that many of these photographs revealed archaeological features which could not be seen at ground level. The outlines of buildings buried beneath the soil, the patterns of drainage ditches which had not been used for a long time and the layouts of old areas of cultivation were all shown clearly on photographs. Since that time, the use of aerial photography in archaeology has developed so much that it is, in many parts of the world, the most important method of discovering and mapping new sites.

Archaeological remains show up from the air in several ways. Slight hollows or mounds caused, for example, by the remains of old ditches, irrigation channels, earthworks or barrows (burial mounds),

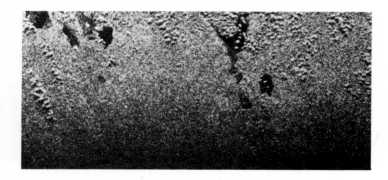

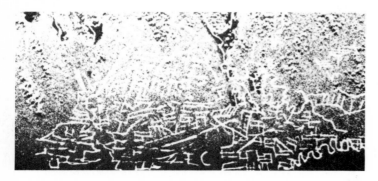

may be emphasized in the shadows cast by the sun when it is low in the sky in the early morning or toward sunset. Photographs taken at these times of day can capture giveaway shadow patterns which, from the ground, do not seem significant.

Buried remains, or traces of earlier human activity now beneath the soil, can affect the growth of plant life above them for thousands of years. Vegetation grows strongly or poorly according to the moisture which reaches its roots. Plants growing above buried masonry and buildings receive less water than those over ordinary soil. Those growing on top of old ditches or pits flourish in the damp soil in these areas. These differences lead to weak or strong growth and reveal themselves in "crop marks." These are lines of lighter or darker vegetation, thicker or thinner growth. They can be seen and photographed from the air. Marks in the color of the topsoil in an area can reveal disturbances caused by building, plowing, or ditching many centuries before. Even the way in which snow or frost melts, or dew settles on the soil, may show up buried walls or other patterns of soil disturbances which cause temperature differences at the surface. By carefully choosing the time of day and the season of the year, and by rephotographing the same area under different growth and weather conditions, archaeologists can build up a complete picture of a site in a way which would be impossible from ground level.

Aerial photography, especially with stereographic cameras which produce a three-dimensional effect,

Canals built by the Mayas in present-day Guatemala, probably in the first century AD, were shown up by an advanced form of radar developed for space research. The original scan (top) when interpreted showed the canals as thin white lines (bottom).

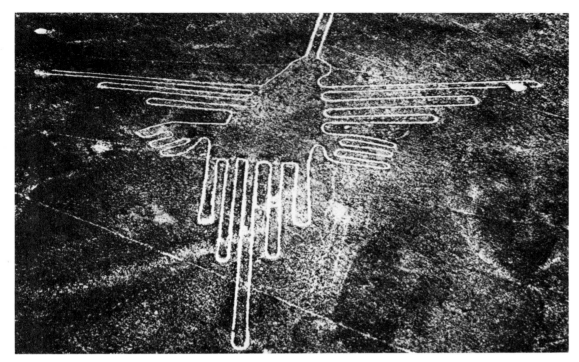

Huge drawings of abstract shapes and animals, such as this hummingbird, were made before 600 AD in the coastal desert of Peru. It is a mystery how the Nazca people set out these designs, which can only be appreciated from the air.

can also be of great help in surveying and mapping large sites and the areas in which they are situated. In recent years infrared photography has been widely used. This can detect small changes in the temperature of the land surface which are caused by the presence of hidden remains beneath it. Although it is normal to use aircraft with either fixed "mapping" cameras or hand-held ones, some archaeologists have ingeniously suspended cameras beneath balloons or kites. This is a cheaper but, of course, also a less controlled form of operation.

At the other extreme, photography by earth satellites is likely to become very important in future years. Satellites can cover every area of the globe. Their sophisticated cameras can now produce pictures almost as clear as those taken by low flying aircraft. Satellite photography, using infrared and other radiation bands invisible to the human eye, will soon be used to detect archaeological remains beneath the sea or hidden under dense forest cover.

An infrared photograph of the Roman town of Calleva Atrebatum, Hampshire, England. The broad lines show the town's streets.

Prospecting for the Past

The aim of all archaeologists is to get information, information about the past. But it is very easy to destroy the evidence, so archaeologists take great care to learn everything they can about a site before starting to dig. As a first stage they study its position in the surrounding countryside. They work out how it fits in with local geology and geomorphology (the study of how the landscape was formed), water supplies and other resources. Next they study the surface of the site, looking for potsherds (which are pieces of broken pottery), stone chippings or any other signs of what lies beneath the ground. In some cases, the way vegetation grows thickly or poorly can show disturbances under the soil and hidden buildings. Earlier finds preserved in local museums or private collections may add useful knowledge of a site before it is dug.

Once this research has been done, archaeologists try to build up a picture of what lies underground and where the important areas are likely to be. Only when they have done this will they feel it is safe to begin digging. Sometimes it is possible to identify the best places to dig by simple methods. The ground can be probed with a long steel rod. If the rod meets an obstacle, hard floors or living areas, for example, may be suspected. Major features, such as walls, can be picked out and mapped in this way. The depth of the remains below the surface can be checked with a hollow drill or auger.

These simple methods of probing and augering take time and can destroy or damage objects. One way of preventing this makes use of the fact that certain remains create small local changes in the earth's magnetic field. Iron objects, fired clay such as pottery, hearths and ovens, some ditches and some types of walls, tombs, and buildings, all give rise to variations. One way to detect these variations is by a proton magnetometer. The protons in hydrogen atoms are made to spin faster by stronger magnetic fields, such as those produced by buildings beneath the soil, and slower by weaker magnetic fields when there are no hidden remains. When a large number of hydrogen protons are affected in this way, the spinning can be shown as an alternating current in an electrical circuit. Changes in a magnetic field can, therefore, be measured as changes in an alternating current.

The first proton magnetometers were very simple. They were bottles of water, containing the hydrogen atoms, surrounded by many coils of thin wire connected to a dial. Now they are more complicated and sensitive. By taking a proton magnetometer over a site, archaeologists can very quickly build up an accurate map of many underground remains. If they are not careful, however, they can as easily be led to a modern sewer system as to a Roman irrigation

A few of the finely carved Etruscan tombs that have been discovered in central Italy with the aid of a resistivity meter.

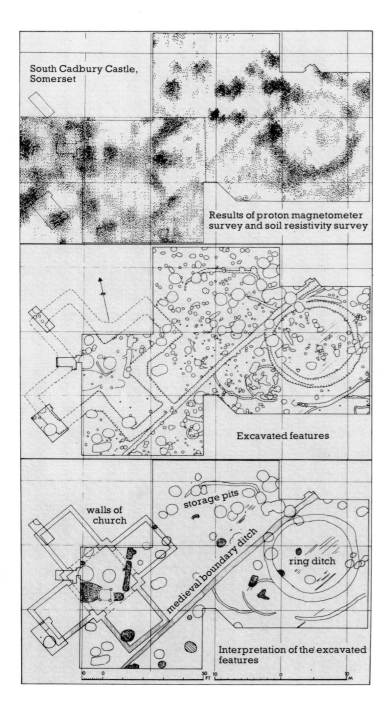

South Cadbury Castle, Somerset

Results of proton magnetometer survey and soil resistivity survey

Excavated features

walls of church

storage pits

medieval boundary ditch

ring ditch

Interpretation of the excavated features

Left: Three stages of a geophysical survey made at South Cadbury, Dorset, England. The top plan shows the site's ground surface before excavation. All finds are plotted on the central plan, while the bottom one shows the different phases of the site's development. The site is marked out with grid lines (above) which are also plotted on the site plan. Machines sensitive to changes in the earth's electrical conductivity are run along the grid lines and the readings marked on the plan.

channel two thousand years old!

Another method of prospecting makes use of the way disturbances in the soil, such as buildings, pits and ditches, produce differing degrees of resistance to the passage of an electrical current. The soil above tombs, walls, and floors, being drier than undisturbed soil, gives a higher resistance reading. Filled-in pits and ditches are damper and give lower resistance than undisturbed soil. A simple form of soil resistivity meter can be made by pushing two metal rods into the ground, connecting a battery across them, and measuring the ratio of the voltage to the current which passes between them. A graph can then be plotted which will show the extremes of resistance, and the archaeologist can excavate in these places.

Modern resistivity meters are far more elaborate but they use the same principle. They are particularly useful in areas where proton magnetometers do not work well, such as those near the magnetic fields set up by power lines. Resistivity surveying has been very useful in finding large numbers of remains quickly. It Italy it was used to pinpoint over ten thousand Etruscan graves and tomb chambers. Little is known about the Etruscans, whom the Romans conquered over 2000 years ago, overwhelming their civilization and language.

The basic method of resistivity surveying has now been developed so that a computer can almost instantly process any changes detected in the soil's resistivity, and plot them on a map.

Excavation: 1

Excavation lies at the heart of archaeology. It provides the archaeologist with the hard facts that are used to check and improve theories and to reconstruct the past. But excavation is expensive and time consuming. More important, it is destructive. Perhaps there is no other way to answer certain questions. Sometimes a site is threatened by highway construction or natural forces, such as floods. But, whatever the reasons, good teamwork between everyone concerned is essential for successful excavation.

Geologists in the eighteenth century had shown how important stratification was in revealing the way the earth had developed, and in helping them date particular layers. Stratification is the way in which rocks and soils in the earth form visible layers, the most recent ones lying on top of the earlier ones. Later archaeologists realized the importance of stratification when it happened on a smaller scale, such as when a group of people inhabited a cave year after year and dropped household rubbish in it, when a grave was filled in, or when one house was built on top of the remains of another. By slicing carefully through the earth, archaeologists could reveal these strata and the objects embedded in them. Each layer, usually of a different color or texture, represents a definite period in the use of that site. Often the depth of the layer can show the length of that period. By identifying and linking the same layers in different areas of a site, archaeologists can prove that different objects found in those strata belong to the same period.

The aim of an excavation is not just to dig up ancient coins or to expose mosaic pavements. It is also to connect finds with particular layers which will show the order in which things happened on that site. Sometimes a whole site is excavated with layer after layer carefully removed. This is, of course, expensive and usually kept for small structures such as huts and burial mounds. At other times digging is kept to a small area, which is either stripped or has rectangular trenches set out across it.

The first stage of excavation is often sheer hard work. Many sites, especially in old towns, are covered

Archaeologists face special difficulties when working in cities. Heavy-duty earth-moving machinery had to be brought in at this site in the City of London to remove existing, more recent foundations before the ancient levels and walls, seen exposed here, could be worked on.

Every find and feature is carefully plotted on scale drawings of the site. Portable grids, with internal strings forming subdivisions, help the archaeologist transfer information accurately from the soil to graph paper.

Checks on stratigraphy are made throughout this excavation at Katmai, Alaska, as layers are removed and new features discovered.

by several yards of rubble and old foundations which must be removed before the real work can begin. In country areas sites are often covered by permanent pasture or by deep top soil, both of which can be stripped off down to the archaeological deposits. Earth-moving machinery and picks and shovels are the tools used in these operations. It is only much later that the highly delicate excavation work, which most people imagine archaeologists doing, comes into the picture.

The site is surveyed and fixed on the best large-scale published map of the area. The director of the excavation must be able to record the exact position, in three dimensions, of anything on the site. Using wooden stakes, nails and string, the excavators lay out an accurately measured grid. Each square marked off has its own reference number, and finds from each square are drawn onto a plan. As the archaeologist digs down into the site, the successive layers

which are uncovered in the vertical trench walls are also carefully drawn to scale on graph paper. These plans and section drawings are as important a part of the evidence as the photographs and finds themselves.

As archaeologists work they destroy much of their evidence. They disturb and remove layers, carry away excavated soil to a waste or spoil heap, and take away finds and soil samples for further study. After the excavation the only evidence which will remain is that in notebooks, drawings, and photographs and, of course, the finds themselves. Archaeologists therefore record everything they do and every aspect of the site. A single seed could tell them that early farmers were cultivating maize long before it was thought likely. The reddish color of burned earth could lead them to the hearth of an Iron Age hut.

Excavation: 2

Now the really painstaking work begins. Trowels, small brushes, and tiny dental tools take the place of picks and shovels. The earth is gently removed from around finds, and delicate items are photographed in position. These may be reinforced with a chemical solution, which when painted on hardens quickly, or by bandaging the object and pouring plaster of Paris around it to make a hard shell. All the excavated earth is sifted through a bank of sieves with graduated meshes to make sure that even the smallest items, such as beads and fishbones, are found. Photographs in color and black and white are taken at every stage of excavation and in different kinds of light.

Pieces of pottery, bone, and worked stone, which need no laboratory treatment, are put in trays or bags labeled with the site's name-code, year, and

Researchers at the British Museum, London, sorting out remains from the wreck of the trading-ship Colossus. Thousands of potsherds had to be sorted and studied before detailed reconstruction could begin.

An archaeological artist making detailed records of the decorated pottery fragments found at an Early Stone Age site at Tešice-Kyjóvice in Czechoslovakia.

layer number. Each excavator has a special tray for the things he or she finds while digging, and must be careful to keep finds from one layer separate from those of the next. At the end of the day, find-trays are taken to the finds shed, where the potsherds are washed, dried and marked with the code in India ink. Small finds, such as coins and glass, are numbered and treated separately. Each is usually measured accurately on the horizontal grid at the site and the position marked on the plan. A detailed diary is kept of all aspects of the dig.

Modern excavation is a matter of teamwork often involving several specialists – animal bone experts and botanists, for example. The work can be done properly only if the director and site foreman have absolute control. The excavators themselves must know exactly what they have to do and how their particular tasks and finds fit into the jigsaw puzzle of the whole excavation. Digging is hard work. It is tiring to spend all day perhaps knee-deep in mud, scrubbing potsherds or sieving excavated soil. But the occasional thrill of unearthing a bronze brooch or of finding a wall-painting compensates for the drudgery.

A fine spray of water clears the earth from fragile bones at an excavation in the City of London.

Preserving Our Past

It is very important to preserve ancient objects after they have been excavated so that they do not crumble or decay any further. They are usually sent to a laboratory but first the excavator makes sure that finds are treated immediately so that they reach the laboratory in the best possible state. Fragile material must be supported and strengthened before or immediately after it is removed from the soil. Wood which has absorbed water becomes soft, heavy, and weakened. It must not be allowed to break under its own weight, or to dry out, as it will then crack and distort. To prevent this it is usually wrapped and kept damp or in water.

When an object has been excavated its condition will depend on a number of things. The most important are the materials of which it is made, the surrounding soil and the length of time it has been buried. In most soil conditions organic materials disappear completely. These are materials, such as wood, paper, and leather, which have been obtained from living organisms. A buried ship, carrying the funeral treasure of a seventh century Anglo-Saxon king, was discovered at Sutton Hoo in Suffolk, England. The wood of which it was made had vanished but impressions, stains, and nails in the soil showed where it had been. On the other hand, organic materials can last well in dry conditions. The hot, dry climate in Egypt has preserved the feather fans and wooden cosmetic boxes of noble ladies who died four thousand years ago. In very damp soil, clay and bone soon become fragile and may fall apart if not carefully dried.

The laboratory treatment of wood from archaeological sites is now highly developed. The main purpose is to replace any water which has been absorbed into the timber by another substance which will not

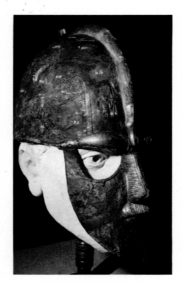

The Sutton Hoo helmet, made in Sweden, was found broken and distorted in the soil. The first reconstruction (right) was made soon after the helmet's discovery. The second reconstruction (far right) is much more accurate.

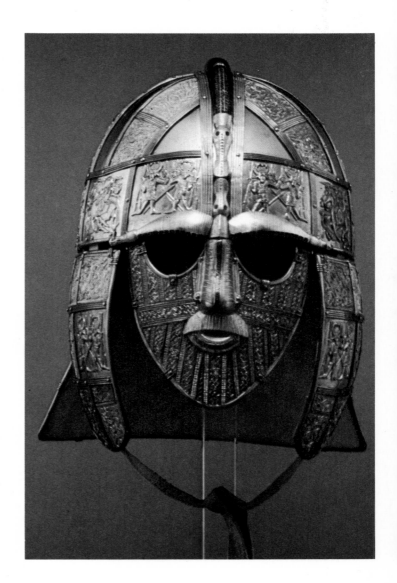

A skilled excavator using water jets unearthed fragile pieces of a unique fifteenth century AD Indian woodcarving at Ozette, Washington. After conservation the object was reconstructed. The sculpture, inlaid with over 600 sea otter teeth, showed the back and dorsal fin of a whale.

damage it. This will strengthen it and prevent the remains from changing shape. The most popular way of doing this is by allowing the wood to slowly absorb polyethylene glycol, a type of wax. Many archaeological specimens, when recovered, contain chemicals in solution which can harm them, especially if crystallization occurs later. In some materials, such as ivory, bone, or stone, these chemicals can be removed by careful washing. Unbaked clay remains, such as cuneiform tablets or waterlogged pottery, are carefully dried in the laboratory and can then be baked. Metal objects frequently suffer in the soil. They may become corroded or, in extreme cases, all the original metal may be changed into another substance. X-ray examination may reveal the shape of the original object and details of how it was made. Deposits caused by corrosion can be removed by chemical and mechanical methods.

Once an object has been treated to stop it from decaying it must be stored safely. Most objects must be kept in surroundings of a dry, even temperature. Ultraviolet light must be kept from textiles which it would fade. The most fragile items may need to be strengthened. This is often done by treating them with special resins, sometimes in a vacuum, to make sure that the strengthening material penetrates as deeply as possible. Objects are usually restored in such a way that the process can be easily reversed. The restored parts are carefully made so that they cannot be confused with the genuine pieces. This system allowed the king's helmet in the Sutton Hoo ship burial to be reconstructed a second time, when it was realized that the first reconstruction was incorrect.

Piecing together the three-dimensional jigsaw puzzle of a broken pot is difficult, time-consuming work. Sherds are often missing, and the smallest mistake can throw the whole vessel askew.

19

Remains from the Earth

Most of an archaeologist's finds are objects made from inorganic, or lifeless, material, such as metal, stone, glass, or pottery. This is because these materials last longer than organic ones. Many scientific techniques have been developed to examine these materials so that they will give up the secrets of their age, origin, and use.

Stone tools are the main evidence of the activities of our oldest known ancestors. Sometimes only the tools are found but occasionally excavators find the sites where they were made. By examining the amount of waste and rejected material at such sites, the way it is scattered and perhaps by trying to make similar tools themselves, they may learn something of the time and effort involved in tool making. On a few sites, excavators may also be able to work out how many people were involved in producing the raw material.

Archaeologists can establish how a tool was used and what it was used on by examining, under a micro-scope, the wear on its edges or point. The origins of a stone artifact can be traced by taking a very thin, translucent slice from it to examine under a microscope. This reveals the characteristic features of the rock from which it was made. These can then be compared with those of material from known sites. In this way carved jade ornaments of the Maya civilization of Central America (300–900 AD) have been traced to particular jade sources, which reveal trading contacts over the whole of Central America.

Pottery is the most common material discovered by archaeologists. It can be dated successfully in modern laboratories. Also, by careful study of its shape and structure and the material from which it is made, a great deal can be discovered about the techniques used to make it and its connection with pottery from other sites. The main ingredients in the clay can be revealed under a microscope and these can be confirmed by spectrometry. This entails vaporizing samples of the clay so that the particular

This carved jade plaque shows a Maya dignitary seated on a throne. It is said to have been found at Teotihuacán, a great city which flourished in central Mexico, hundreds of miles away from the Maya homeland. Such archaeological finds hint at long-distance diplomatic and trade contacts, and these are being proved by excavations in the Maya quarter of Teotihuacán.

Maya sites in Central America. Precious apple-green jade was traded hundreds of miles from its source in the Motagua River, Guatemala, to great Maya cities such as Tikal and Uxmal.

This corroded, shapeless lump of metal was found in a grave in southern England.

When X-rayed, it proved to be an inlaid Anglo-Saxon buckle.

wavelengths of light given out by each element in it can be recorded. Each element has its own wavelength which identifies it immediately. Some kinds of Japanese and Chinese pottery have been studied by this method. Although there were many beautiful vases in museums, no one knew with certainty from where they came. Now this has been worked out by comparing the clays they were made from with potsherds from excavations in the Far East.

Faults or joints may show up in metal objects when they are X-rayed which suggest how they were made. The structure of a metal object, how it was made and how it was allowed to cool, can be revealed by polishing a small area, etching this with acid and examining it under a microscope. X-rays and spectrometry are used to identify the elements present in a metal so that the ore they originally came from can be traced. Many careful examinations must be made in a laboratory to build up a picture of the changes in metal working in the distant past.

About four thousand years ago, the Beaker people (so named because of their distinctive clay beaker-shaped pots) migrated from continental Europe to Britain. They used short, flat daggers made of almost pure copper. Later the Wessex people of southern Britain learned to make bronze, an alloy of tin and copper, which is hard and long-lasting. They put the ideal twelve per cent of tin into their beautiful tapering daggers, which greatly improved the strength.

Obsidian, a volcanic glass, was one material that was traded widely in the distant past. It was used for making razor-sharp blades and spear- and arrowheads. In recent years, archaeologists have tried to date obsidian artifacts by using the fact that a freshly made obsidian surface will slowly take up water from its surroundings. This makes a layer that can be measured so that the artifact's age can be worked out fairly accurately. Chemical and other analyses of obsidian can indicate where it came from. This can help to build up a picture of ancient trade routes.

Clues from Plants

Plant foods have always been an important part of the human diet, although not many human groups have ever been entirely vegetarian. Plants and trees are also used by people for many other purposes, such as for clothing, building, weapons, basketry, and dyes. Vegetable material rots quickly in most conditions. Yet in some others, such as peat bogs or very dry places, it survives for thousands of years. Where it is preserved, it can throw light not only on what our ancestors ate but also on what they did. Most important of all, perhaps, it can tell us about the environment in which all this took place and how, over time, our ancestors changed their surroundings.

Plant remains do not just provide clues to the diet of earlier peoples. They also tell us whether they were collecting wild or growing domesticated plants, or even how far they roamed to get their food. The remains of food from plants are preserved in many ways. In Egypt, dried seeds have been recovered from tombs and storage pits, and from the intestines of mummies. Coprolites (fossilized or dried feces)

also contain undigested parts of food plants which can be identified. Dried coprolites were examined from the site at Huaca Prieta on the desert coast of Peru. It seems that the inhabitants, who lived there four thousand years ago, ate mainly beans, squash, and starchy roots, with some mussels and small sea creatures, such as crabs, for delicacies. Occasionally, scraps of food are found which contain recognizable grains, such as wheat and barley.

Plant remains also provide us with other evidence, such as the time of year at which a particular site was used. A large number of peach stones found on an excavation would hint that the site was inhabited during the months of May and June. Contact between various places can be proved as, for example, when corn and tobacco were introduced into Africa from the Americas in the early sixteenth century.

Recovering plant remains is now an essential part of excavation. It is sometimes possible to identify large seeds or the shells of nuts by the naked eye, but often vegetable remains are too small for this. In

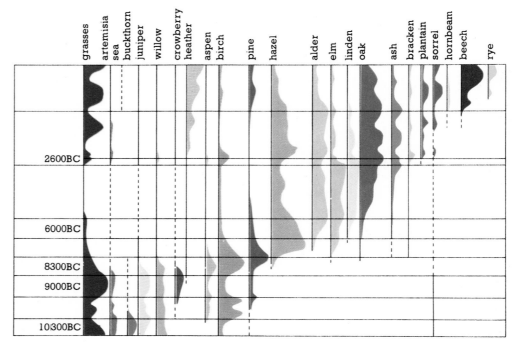

Analysis of pollen samples taken from different layers of an archaeological site can build up a picture of what was growing in the area thousands of years ago, and how the vegetation was affected by human activity. This pollen diagram shows vegetational changes in Jutland, Denmark. The colored parts show the relative amounts of pollen found, the solid lines indicate that traces were found but were too small to quantify, and the dotted lines show that archaeologists think that a particular species may have existed but that no evidence has been found.

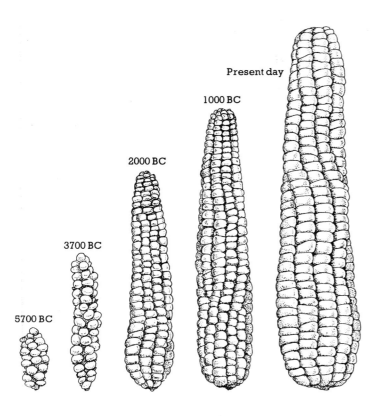

In the Tehuacán valley, Mexico, archaeologists have found evidence of the prehistoric domestication of corn. The earliest type of cob found was a primitive form, close to its tiny wild ancestor. Later examples show that people were cultivating corn and gradually improving it by careful breeding. Here early types are compared to a cob of modern field corn (all drawn approximately half life size).

Present day

1000 BC

2000 BC

3700 BC

5700 BC

recent years, archaeologists have developed ways of floating these, which are usually light, out of the soil of a site. This can be done by putting the dried soil in water, agitating it, and then scooping off what floats to the top to be examined later. This is done by a seed machine. It consists of a large tank containing water with a frothing agent, similar to dishwashing liquid, and a bubbler unit which pumps air into the water, making it bubble. The seeds then float to the surface.

Each plant or tree produces its own particular form of pollen which can be identified under a microscope. This pollen is produced in large quantities and spreads out from the plant, often over a wide area. Luckily for the archaeologist it is the toughest part of the plant. By building up a picture of the types of pollen from a site or from one layer in a site, archaeologists can discover which trees and plants were growing in the area during the period when the site was occupied. By seeing how pollen types change over time, they can discover how the vegetation changed and work out how much this was due to human activity. For example, if tree pollens decline and pollens from grasses increase, then early farmers may have been clearing the forest to cultivate the land.

Other alterations can suggest great changes in the climate and vegetation, for example, the coming of ice ages and the warmer periods that followed them. Pollen analysis of a Neanderthal cave burial at Shanidar, Iraq, showed that at least eight different kinds of plants had been placed around the corpse, including daisies, groundsel, and hollyhock.

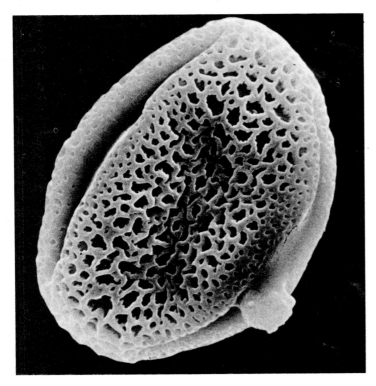

Every plant produces unique identifiable pollen grains. This pollen grain from a Scots pine has been magnified many hundreds of times.

Digging up Bones

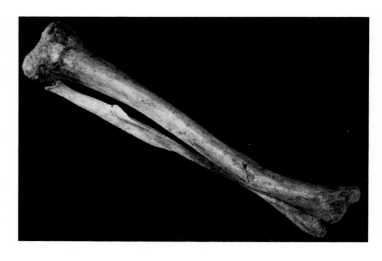

Bones can tell us about accidents and illnesses that befell their owners. Above is a spiral fracture of the lower leg.

There is a grisly fascination about watching an excavator brush the soil away from a skeleton. Complete skeletons are not often found in excavations, but even fragments of bones can be made to reveal clues to the past.

Human bones find their way into the earth in many ways, some deliberate, some accidental. Bodies may be buried carefully in graves, tumbled into pits or fall accidentally down shafts. A corpse may be partly cremated and the bones then buried, or the flesh allowed to rot so the skull or jaw-bone can be kept as a trophy or memorial. Animal bones may be buried in rubbish dumps, left behind by hunters after the meat has been butchered, or buried by rockfalls.

The excavator's first job is to uncover the bones carefully in the earth. When these have been broken and jumbled this is not always easy. If they have become fossilized, the surrounding rock may have to be cut or dissolved away. Some may need to be strengthened before they are lifted. Damp, newly excavated bone will often harden if allowed to dry slowly. Excavating skeletons is slow, painstaking work and archaeologists must record every bone.

Detective work begins as they try to work out from the position of a corpse whether it was buried carefully or pushed hurriedly into a shallow hole. Were bone fractures caused before or after death? There is

This well-preserved corpse of a man who died about 2000 years ago was found in a bog at Tollund, Denmark. He wore a conical leather cap, and the tight noose around his neck suggests that he was murdered. Analysis of his stomach contents showed that he had eaten porridge flavored with herbs as his last meal.

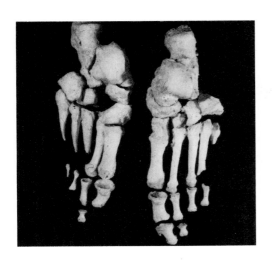

These deformed bones show the crippling effects of leprosy on the feet.

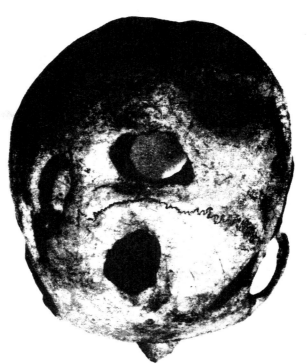

The skull of an ancient Peruvian who died about 3000 years ago. The holes were made during the dangerous operation called trephining.

evidence that live burial was practiced in Ancient Egypt and China. In the Anglo-Saxon period (400–650 AD) in England, women were sometimes buried alive with dead men. Archaeologists have found graves containing twisted female skeletons lying on top of male skeletons and pinned down by large rocks. Some skeletons may have been deliberately laid out in a particular direction, according to the custom of certain groups of people. For example, Christians traditionally were buried facing toward the east.

Bones which are not fossilized can be dated by measuring how much radioactive carbon they contain. The ages of bones which are found in the same cemetery can be checked against each other by the fluorine test. Most water contains fluorine which bones will absorb if they lie in damp soil long enough. By working out the amount of fluorine in bones from the same site, we can see if they were buried at the same time. This method was used to prove that the supposedly prehistoric skull found at Piltdown in Sussex, England in 1912 was a fake. The tests made some forty years later showed that the skull contained 0.1 per cent fluorine while the jaw-bone contained about 0.03 per cent fluorine. This proved that the jaw was much more recent than the skull.

Dating bones gives some idea of the age of a site. Close examination of human bones also tells us much about their former owners, at what age they died, and their sex – in general the bones of males are larger and heavier than those of females. The extent and pattern of wear in the teeth may reveal not only the age of the owners but also the type of food they ate. Dental decay increased rapidly when people became farmers and started eating more cereals. Damage to the bones may show what diseases they suffered from, and sometimes it is possible to decide what caused death. Occasionally, a skull may show that the owner was operated upon during his life. One Peruvian skull, about three thousand years old, shows that no fewer than seven disks of bone had been cut away. Bone had grown around the edges of the holes later, which proved that the victim had survived all these operations!

If several skeletons are found, it is possible to say something about the range of ages and number of men and women in a group of people. The shape of the body and particularly the skull can tell us about relationships with other groups.

There are usually more animal than human bones found on a site. By studying these, we can picture which animals were hunted for food and which were domesticated. Marks made on the bones will show what methods the early hunters used to kill their prey and how they then butchered the meat.

The Carbon 14 Revolution

Dating finds is one of the archaeologist's greatest problems. It is sometimes possible to estimate dates of finds when they are unearthed in the same layer as objects whose dates are known, such as coins. But some ancient societies produced no helpful objects and for many years dates and chronologies could only be estimated.

Many scientific techniques have been discovered during this century to date archaeological finds accurately. A revolution in dating happened in 1947 when an American scientist, Willard Libby, proved that we could establish to within a fairly narrow time-margin the age of almost all organic materials – substances such as wood, charcoal, bone, flax, antler, and peat – which were once part of living organisms. This could be done by working out how much of a particular sort of radioactive carbon was contained in these materials. This form of carbon is usually referred to as radiocarbon, or carbon 14.

Live plants absorb carbon 14, together with the non-radioactive carbon 12, in more or less equal amounts from the atmosphere. Animals that eat the plants also absorb these two sorts of carbon. But when a living organism dies it no longer absorbs carbon. The carbon 14 already in its tissues or cells begins to decay, or lose its radioactivity. The rate at which the decay occurs is known. After about 5730 years ± 40 years (the plus or minus gives room for error), about half the radioactivity is left. This is known as the "half-life." Carbon 12, however, does not decay like carbon 14, and it is the comparison between the two which enables archaeologists to date an object. By measuring the proportion of carbon 14 to carbon 12 in any organic material, we can work out how much carbon 14 has disappeared since the organism died, and therefore how long ago it died.

Carbon 14 dating is usually expressed as plus or minus so many years BP, or "Before Present," which, for convenience, is taken as 1950. A human bone, for example, may be dated as 2000 ± 100 BP, which would be 2100 to 1900 years before the present. This would mean between 150 BC and 50 AD. Therefore, by dating the archaeological find we can, with care, date the layer in which it was found.

Radiocarbon dating has transformed ideas about the pattern of our prehistory. Many archaeological remains have been dated to periods far older than anyone had imagined. In Britain, it was long thought that the great circular monument at Stonehenge had

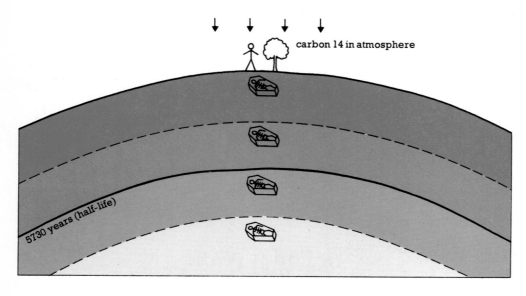
carbon 14 in atmosphere

5730 years (half-life)

Radioactive carbon is absorbed by all plants and animals. When they die, the carbon 14 stored in them begins to decay at a known rate. After 5730 years only half the radioactive carbon is left. Measurement of the radiocarbon content can therefore date organic material such as wood and rope.

At Stonehenge, above, shallow carvings of daggers, seen below, on a massive vertical slab may date to the time of Mycenae, 3500 years ago.

been constructed in about 1600 BC by native barbarian tribes who were inspired by the early Greek civilization of Mycenae. The discovery of carvings of Mycenaean type daggers on one of the upright stones seemed to confirm this. But carbon 14 tests showed that the first monument built at Stonehenge, an earthen bank, was begun by 2500 BC and the stone circles were completed by 2000 BC. The civilization at Mycenae did not flower until about 1600 BC and so, even at this time, Stonehenge was an ancient monument. Perhaps a Mediterranean trader carved the daggers on the stone to mark his visit.

Unfortunately, the amount of carbon 14 present in the atmosphere, and available to be absorbed into living things, has varied over the years. This may have been due partly to changes in the earth's

magnetic field. The widespread burning of fossil fuels, such as coal and oil, in the last two centuries has reduced the amount of carbon 14 in the atmosphere, while the recent testing of atomic weapons has increased it. For these reasons research into radiocarbon dating is still going on. Nevertheless, this method has given the archaeologist a tool of great power and many objects and sites have been securely dated by it.

Split-twig figurine found at the Grand Canyon. It has been carbon dated to 1000 BC.

Tree-ring Dating

This section through the trunk of an oak shows the annual growth rings.

Archaeologists continue to seek new, accurate ways to date things. In the last sixty years, they have realized that the patterns of rings in trees may be of great help in fixing a date to archaeological sites in which wood is found.

As a tree grows, it adds a new ring each year. At the start of each growing season a tree produces a layer of large cells beneath its bark. As the season continues and winter draws near, these become smaller and smaller until growth almost stops. Then, next spring, large cells again begin to form next to the bark. It is this continuous process that produces the characteristic pattern of rings in a tree. It helps us to distinguish one year's growth from the next. But the pattern of growth is not the same in each year. In dry years the tree will grow slowly and its annual growth ring will be thin, while wet years will be reflected in increased growth and thicker rings. The pattern of rings in a tree thus summarizes the climate of the tree's lifetime.

If we cut down a living tree, we can find out how old it is by counting the number of the rings inward from the bark to the center. The outermost ring represents the present year, and the center represents the year of its first growth. Now if the tree rings show a recognizable patterning, for example two years of thin growth together occurring twenty-nine and thirty years ago (which indicate two years of dry weather), we can look for the same pattern in the rings of other trees. Suppose we found the same pattern in the two outer rings of one of those trees, we would know that that tree died twenty-nine years ago. By comparing the overlapping of distinctive growth ring patterns we can, with care and luck, construct a master pattern for growth rings going back many hundreds of years. Archaeologists learned to compare the pattern of growth rings in timber they had found in the old beams or posts of houses with the master pattern. They could then date the timber and so gain some idea of the age of the archaeological site. This

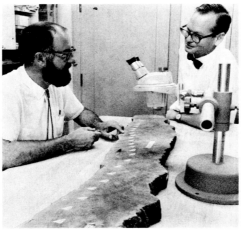

A researcher takes a core sample of wood from a bristlecone pine (far left). It will be carefully prepared, mounted and studied at the Laboratory of Tree Ring Research, University of Arizona (left), along with many other such samples. Recognizable patterns of tree ring growth are correlated and gradually a master pattern for dendrochronological dating is built up.

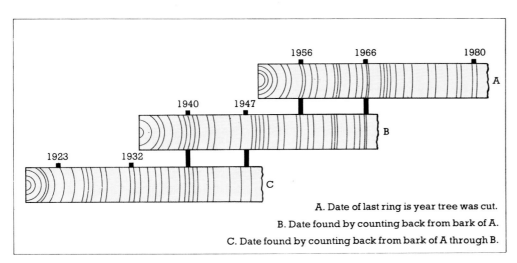

A. Date of last ring is year tree was cut.
B. Date found by counting back from bark of A.
C. Date found by counting back from bark of A through B.

Annual growth rings on a tree are easy to identify. The pattern of growth varies according to climatic conditions and where the same patterns can be identified in different trees of different ages it is possible to build up a master pattern extending far back into the past.

method of dating timber is called dendrochronology.

However, there are certain complications in dating by this method. The pattern of growth rings varies if the trees are of different species and if they live in different environments. Where there are dramatic changes in temperature and rainfall over a short distance, ring patterns may vary greatly. Damage to a tree's top branches and leaves will also affect the cells it produces during a year.

To extend a master pattern back into history from trees alive now, there have to be examples of timber preserved from the past which overlap without a break. In northern Europe, oak trees can live for up to five hundred years and after cutting the wood is very long-lasting. It was often used in the construction of

buildings and has provided a most useful set of ring patterns. But recently, the most important work has been done with the bristlecone pine. These trees grow at about 10,000 feet in California and can live for over 4000 years. When dead, the wood is highly resistant to decay and damage by insects. From trees like this scientists have now built up a master pattern of tree rings dating back about 9000 years.

Radiocarbon dating can be checked against timber dated by dendrochronology. However, it is important to discover how long the timber had been dead before it was used because otherwise an inaccurate date would be obtained. There is no master pattern for areas where wood is scarce or where little is preserved because of a hot and humid climate.

Other Dating Methods

The radiocarbon method can be used to date materials up to about 70,000 years old. However, after 50,000 years the method becomes inaccurate as less and less carbon 14 remains in the object being examined. Another technique, the potassium-argon method (also based on radioactive decay), is used to date materials from very remote periods in history, sometimes as far back as ten million years ago. But it can only be used on volcanic rocks.

Potassium is one of the most common elements in the earth's composition and a very small amount of it is radioactive. This potassium, potassium 40, decays at a known rate to produce calcium and the gas argon 40. The half-life of potassium 40 is about 1.3 billion years. Scientists can measure how much potassium 40 and argon 40 are left in a piece of rock. They can then work out how long the potassium has been decaying and, therefore, how old the rock is. The older the rock, the more argon it will contain and the less potassium. The remains of the earliest hominids (manlike creatures) were found embedded in layers of volcanic rock in the Rift valley of East Africa. By dating each rock layer, archaeologists found the fossil remains to be over three million years old.

Potsherds are the most common archaeological find in most parts of the world. For many years, archaeologists compared pots, their shapes, surface decorations, and the composition of the clay from which they were made, to decide from which period they came. But what was needed was some method whereby these pots could be dated absolutely, in calendar years. Pots are usually broken within a few years of being made, and so this would help archaeologists to date the layers in which potsherds were found.

In the last twenty years a method of doing this has been developed. This method is called thermoluminescence. It depends on the fact that the clay from which pottery is made contains electrons which have absorbed energy from radioactive elements in the soil. When the pot is fired, this energy is given off as light and the electrons return to their normal state.

However, they start reabsorbing radioactivity and so the energy level increases again. Eventually, the pot is broken, thrown away and probably covered by other rubbish. Over the years, as it lies buried in the ground, minute amounts of radioactive elements

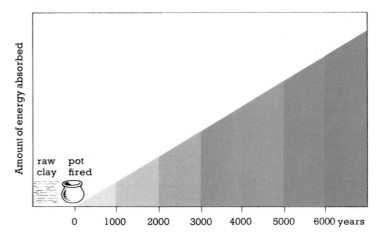

This diagram shows how dating using thermoluminescence works. Electrons in the fired clay gradually absorb energy as it ages. This can be measured as light and an absolute date can be obtained.

This diagram shows the theory behind potassium-argon dating. Volcanic rocks contain radioactive potassium, which decays at a known rate. Measurement of the radioactivity can date layers millions of years old.

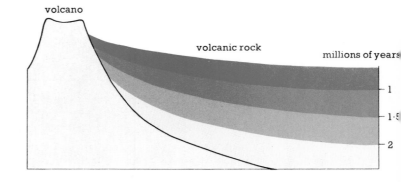

Olduvai Gorge, Tanzania, is part of the African Rift valley. It is famous for the early hominid remains which have been found there by the British anthropologists Louis and Mary Leakey. The remains were dated by the potassium-argon method.

continue to be absorbed. The older the pot, the more energy the electrons in the clay will contain. Archaeologists discovered that if the pot were reheated after being unearthed, the energy would appear as light which could be measured. In this way, the time since the pot was originally fired could be calculated.

Thermoluminescence has also been widely used to identify fakes. Some Greek statuettes and Peruvian pots, which came into museum collections over a hundred years ago, have recently proved to be copies of the real thing. Experimental research is still going on into this technique and it is a valuable check on radiocarbon dating.

Tests on potsherds from the deep cave system of the Cueva de los Tayos, in Ecuador, gave a date of 3450 ± 397 BP. This compared well with a radiocarbon date taken from seashells found in the same layer. The decorative seashells had been carried from the Pacific Ocean across the Andes and down into sacred caves in the Amazon jungle, possibly by pilgrims or traders, about 3000 years ago.

Fakes and Frauds

In 1912 Charles Dawson, an English lawyer and amateur archaeologist, found fragments of a skull, apparently of the same form as that of modern man (*Homo sapiens sapiens*), close to an apelike jawbone and teeth. He discovered them near Piltdown, in Sussex. The "ape" jaw fitted the human skull and the wear on the teeth indicated the creature had eaten a diet similar to that of humans. Nearby were found remains of extinct animals, dateable to about half a million years ago, and also some crude stone tools. The long sought-after "missing link" between us and our apelike ancestors seemed to have been found. More remarkable remains were found in the area in 1915, and eventually it was accepted that Piltdown Man was a most important early hominid.

It was not until 1953 that scientific techniques proved the whole thing was bogus. Fluorine levels in the cranium and jaw were different, and radiocarbon tests later showed that the cranium dated to the thirteenth century AD. The jaw was from a modern ape and had been dyed, and the teeth had been filed down to the required shape and dyed. The fossil remains had been planted to back up the supposed age of the skull.

Who faked Piltdown Man is still uncertain. Perhaps it was a joke or to show how easily hoodwinked leading scientists could be, or perhaps to support a particular theory of evolution or to bring fame to the finder: no one really knows. The motive for other fakes is sometimes clearer. In the United States fakes have been "discovered" which seem to show that Phoenicians and Vikings from the Old World had traveled far inland long before the time of Columbus and had erected inscribed stone monuments.

Archaeology and faking are almost inseparable. Sometimes real or fake material is inserted into an

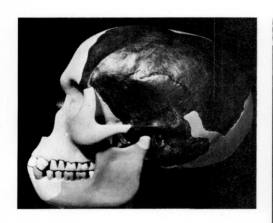

The Piltdown skull (above). The darkened parts are casts of the pieces actually excavated. Right: At the Piltdown site are (left to right): Teilhard de Chardin, Charles Dawson, a laborer, and Arthur Woodward from the British Museum (Natural History). Some people believe that de Chardin joined in the hoax.

WORKERS AT PILTDOWN.

This baked clay tablet from Glozel, France, is inscribed in an unknown script which has links with Latin, Phoenician and Iberian alphabets. Is it a fake or a genuine artifact?

Terra-cotta Nok head from northern Nigeria. It has been radiocarbon dated to about 300 BC. The Nok people were probably the first iron-smelters in West Africa.

archaeological site to which it does not belong. This is called "salting" and goes back to Boucher de Perthes' excavations in France in the 1830s. There, the workmen, knowing visitors liked to see discoveries being made, planted genuine stone hand-axes and fossilized animal bones in places where they could hit upon them at promising moments.

During the 1920s many archaeologists became suspicious of discoveries at Glozel in France. Here excavators claimed to have found items of Paleolithic (Old Stone Age) art, as well as an unknown form of writing. Investigations on the spot suggested that someone was secretly burying fake material in the site and placing it in layers which indicated it had great age. The pieces looked like modern fakes and were ignored until a few years ago when thermoluminescence tests set their age at about 2000 years. The Glozel puzzle has acquired a new lease of life. Salting is usually noticeable. It is very hard to insert objects into layers in a way which cannot be spotted.

Another kind of faking is done to make money. The objects recovered by archaeologists are sometimes beautiful or rare. If they came on the market they would be easily sold to collectors or museums. The faker steps in to meet this demand. Such fakes are a great nuisance to archaeologists. If they are not spotted they may lead scholars to come to entirely wrong conclusions. In recent years, a number of fake terra-cotta (baked clay) human heads, in the style of the Nok culture of West Africa, have been reported. These are claimed to be about 2000 years old and to have been smuggled out of Nigeria. Their form is different from true Nok pieces. If they were genuine, archaeologists would have to revise their ideas about the development of Nok art styles.

Fakes are easier to spot after a lapse of time. Scientists develop new techniques or learn more about the archaeology of the areas from which objects are supposed to come. When this happens the fakes begin to stand out. They do not fit in with genuine material and the scholar notices mistakes in their manufacture or design. If the suspected objects are closely examined, they will often show evidence of manufacturing techniques unknown to the ancient craftsmen. Nevertheless, fakes and faking continue to be a hazard to the archaeologist.

Historical Archaeology

Much of archaeology is concerned with prehistory, which archaeologists define as the time before writing was invented in any society. History really begins with the existence of written documents. In Mesopotamia, which had one of the earliest civilizations, history begins about five thousand years ago. In some other parts of the world, the prehistoric period lasted almost until the present day. Considering the three million or so years human beings have existed, all history is very recent.

Archaeologists have always made the best use they can of written records to understand what our ancestors thought and did. Inscriptions on Egyptian tombs, signs on Maya monuments, and royal proclamations made by Indian rulers, such as Aśoka in the third century BC, have all thrown light on remains from those periods.

The decrees of Aśoka were inscribed on rock surfaces and specially erected pillars in places where people gathered. They were a sort of public notice. The writings explained the peaceful Buddhist ways which he wished his people to follow. They also list his good deeds.

"On the roads I have planted banyan trees, which will give shade to beasts and man. I have had many groves of mangoes planted and I have had wells dug . . ."

The archaeologist and the historian who study our recorded past must have a good understanding of each other's needs when work on a site is progressing. Every possible piece of useful information needs to be extracted from whatever is available. There may be old building accounts, plans, maps, court records, charters, rental agreements, and tax returns. Any of these may provide useful clues.

The archaeologist can then enlarge the picture of the past presented by written records and bring it to life. In England, for example, there have been interesting excavations at York and Winchester. In these and other digs, many new discoveries have added to the information provided by the records of the city, the charters, bills of sale, church records, old maps, and the inscriptions on tombs. At Win-chester archaeologists were able to show the surprising fact that the grid pattern of the town streets belonged to a later period than they had previously supposed. It was of Anglo-Saxon and not Roman origin. Such excavations have revealed ordinary details of everyday life which were taken for granted and not recorded in the written documents. The

One of the pillars erected by King Aśoka. It stands at Vaisali, in Bihar, possibly overlooking the grave of Ananda, one of Aśoka's disciples. Only one other of these pillars remains in India.

Leather shoe from the Coppergate excavations, York, England, it dates from the tenth century AD.

design and working methods of small shops and workshops have been investigated. At Coppergate in York, a complete Viking leather-working shop has been preserved in waterlogged soil. Equipment for curing, stretching and cutting leather has been found together with many half-complete shoes and purses.

Excavations in Australia have told us much about life in the early colonial settlements there. They have provided the sort of information which never would have been written down about contact between the aborigines and white settlers.

Excavations at Fort Toulouse in Alabama have produced many examples of the trade goods brought by the French colonists in the eighteenth century. These give us a lot of information about what types of guns were being used and what kind of alcohol was supplied to the Creek Indian confederacy. Broken gin bottles, bits and pieces of gunlock plates, bullet molds, and gunflints are all that now remain.

Outstanding work has been carried out at Williamsburg, Jamestown, and Yorktown in Virginia. Here the records of early colonial settlements have been used as a basis of large-scale excavations and reconstructions. Visitors to Williamsburg, capital of Virginia from 1699 to 1780, may catch a glimpse of everyday life in eighteenth century America. They can walk through the old town and its gardens, both accurately restored, and see the local inhabitants dressed in the costumes of the period. None of this would have been possible if historians and archaeologists had not worked together to re-create a bygone age.

Finds from the marvelously preserved Oseberg ship burial excavated in southern Norway in 1904 included this beautifully carved four-wheeled wooden carriage. This burial, which dates from 850–900 AD, provided many details about the Vikings' everyday life which are not mentioned in their historical sagas.

A badge worn by a Roman slave: the inscription is a warrant for the slave's arrest if he ran away.

Economic Archaeology

The greatest needs of both people and animals are to find food and to reproduce themselves and prehistoric peoples were no exception. The first archaeologists concentrated upon finding and studying the objects such as pots, brooches, and tools left by prehistoric peoples. They were not really concerned with the economic bases of the societies. Instead, they took artifacts as their foundation and worked out systems to explain the technological development of ancient societies. These systems were based on the three principal materials used to make tools and weapons. Archaeologists still talk about the Stone, Bronze and Iron Ages. But today we are increasingly interested in **how** prehistoric groups lived, and ask many questions about how early groups related to and were affected by their geographical environment.

One of the first excavations to use this approach was that at Star Carr, Yorkshire, England. This Mesolithic (Middle Stone Age) site was chosen because it was thought to contain well-preserved organic remains. These would help archaeologists to reconstruct the economy of the people who had lived there nine thousand years ago. A team of geologists, botanists and zoologists worked together with archaeologists in order to extract every possible scrap of evidence from the excavation.

The site at Star Carr, occupied at about 7500 BC, produced many stone and bone tools and showed that the inhabitants had worked antlers to make hunting and fishing gear. The remains of a wooden paddle were found, indicating that they built small boats to use on the nearby lake. Thousands of finds of animal bones, plant remains, and pollen grains were carefully studied in laboratories. By fitting together all the different pieces of information, it was possible to say that the site was occupied from late autumn to early spring by about twenty-five people. They came back to Star Carr every year for about twenty years, and lived on a log platform which they built on the edge of the lake.

Anthropologists have gathered detailed information about hunting peoples of the last century, such as some tribes of American Indians. This has helped archaeologists to guess much about the Star Carr people. They probably ranged over about 200 square miles of territory containing about 3400 red deer. This was a plentiful supply of meat for the four or five family groups that lived there. Some of the deer stag skulls found in the excavations had been made into headdresses. These might have been used by hunters stalking game or worn for ceremonial dances.

Human societies and ways of life have been greatly affected by their geographical environments. On the other hand, many peoples have tried to improve their surroundings by drainage or irrigation schemes, and so themselves have molded their own environ-

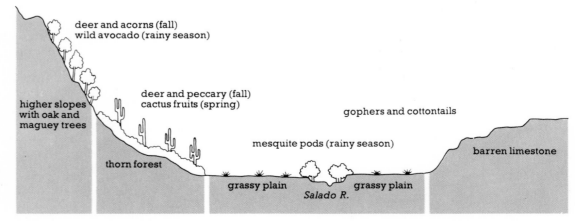

This section through the Tehuacán valley, Mexico, shows wild food resources – the plants and animals which were most plentiful for early settlers at certain seasons of the year. The people lived on the grassy river plain in the rainy season (May to November), and followed the game to higher ground in drier periods.

deer and acorns (fall)
wild avocado (rainy season)

deer and peccary (fall)
cactus fruits (spring)

higher slopes with oak and maguey trees

gophers and cottontails

mesquite pods (rainy season)

thorn forest

barren limestone

grassy plain

Salado R.

grassy plain

This wall painting from an Egyptian tomb of 1500 BC shows just how far Ancient Egypt's trade links stretched. These from Punt (modern Ethiopia) are carrying ostrich eggs and a myrrh tree. Myrrh was an important incense in the ancient world.

At Grimes Graves in Norfolk, England, Neolithic miners dug deep shafts to reach layers of high quality flint. Flints from these mines have been found in Europe, which helps archaeologists to understand the trade and economy of this Neolithic society.

ment. The archaeologists studying the pattern of human settlement in an area try to discover what supplies of raw material and foodstuffs were within reasonable reach of the village or cave being investigated. Using this method, archaeologists traced the pattern of human settlement in the Virú valley of northern Peru from five thousand years ago to the present day. They often begin such a study by walking over every part of the landscape surrounding the main settlement site. They note all the different types of landform, soil, vegetation, and animal life. They also locate water supplies, rock and mineral outcrops, and cave and rock shelters. Minutely detailed studies based on this kind of information are called site catchment analyses.

Underwater Archaeology

It was a terrible disaster when, in 1628, the great vessel Wasa sank suddenly in Stockholm harbor as she set out on her maiden voyage. For the archaeologist, however, it has meant a wonderful insight into life aboard a ship of that period. In 1961, after great effort, the vessel was raised again to the surface. The cabins and hold had filled with mud which had preserved many of the contents. Skeletons were found, fully clothed, their purses full of coins. The structure of the ship provided valuable evidence of seventeenth century methods of shipbuilding.

Underwater archaeology is a new subject. Like all archaeology, it must be very carefully recorded. Until recently this was almost impossible, as archaeologists could hardly venture beneath the water. Clumsy early diving suits needed air pumped from the surface. A very simple form of underwater excavation took place in 1904, when offerings to a rain god were dredged up from a sacred Maya pool at Chichén Itzá in Mexico. There were treasures of jade and gold as well as the bones of forty-one people who, apparently, had been sacrificed. However, it was not until 1942 that the Aqualung was invented and archaeologists could suddenly penetrate depths with ease.

Material comes to be under water in many ways. Parts of the Mediterranean sea routes are littered with shipwrecks of many periods. Sometimes earthquakes and landslides may cause sites to sink under water. In other areas rising sea levels or sinking land, or the creation of new artificial lakes submerge sites. Some items are thrown into the water as offerings. The famous Iron Age Battersea shield may have found its way into the Thames River as an offering to a water god.

Each type of underwater deposit presents its own problems. When wrecks break up, their cargo and structure may be spread over a wide area, continually worn away and shifted by tides and storms. In warm

A specially trained archaeologist wearing an Aqualung investigates a shipwreck in tropical waters off Singapore.

climates they may become covered with corals and other marine growths. In some regions heavy objects sink deep into silt which both preserves and hides them.

The methods used for excavation on land are specially adapted for underwater excavation. The archaeologist usually lays out a horizontal reference grid of wires or metal rods and measures vertical positions with surveying instruments.

The Battersea Shield (left), found in the Thames at Battersea, London, is a fine example of Celtic craftmanship. It dates from about 100 BC to 100 AD and is made from one piece of bronze. The three roundels, which have inlaid enamel decoration, were made separately and riveted onto the main piece.

The Swedish warship Wasa sank off Stockholm in 1628 and lay forgotten until rescue work began in 1956. She was lifted into shallow water in 1959 (below left). Then, in April 1961, she was raised to the surface (below). The water was pumped out and she was towed to a special dock for restoration.

It is difficult to excavate under water. Disturbed deposits cloud the water and quickly settle back again. Mud or sand and small finds can often be removed by using an air hose. Air is pumped down the outer sleeve of a long tube and bubbles back to the surface up the center, taking with it the mud and small objects. Large objects may be raised by attaching them to bags or balloons, which are then filled with air so they float up to the surface.

Not all underwater archaeology involves diving. When five Viking vessels were discovered in Roskilde Fjord, Denmark, a special sort of walled dam was built around them. Then the water in which they lay was pumped away so they could be recorded and recovered.

Underwater archaeology, like that on land, often involves piecing together scattered and damaged fragments. At times it is the vessel itself, at others its cargo. The rescue of a cargo began off the Scilly Islands in the English Channel a few years ago. Divers worked on the sailing ship *Colossus*, wrecked in 1798 while carrying to England hundreds of ancient Greek vases for an English nobleman. Material once excavated on land was now being re-excavated under water. Many fragments of this great collection have now been recovered and are slowly being pieced together.

The methods used in underwater archaeology are still being developed. The evidence lying submerged fills many gaps in the story told by dry-land archaeology.

Industrial Archaeology

Until the Industrial Revolution of the eighteenth and nineteenth centuries, most goods were produced by human or animal energy. Then the steam engine was invented. Other sources of power were developed that speeded up production. Soon great quantities of standardized goods, made by machines, were flooding out from the factories of Europe and America. Vast new industrial cities sprang up almost overnight, near to essential iron, water and coal. As mass-production increased, new natural resources were discovered and developed. Communication between peoples and countries grew rapidly. Soon almost all parts of the world became linked in a vast trading network. The rate of change accelerated and the gap between industrialized societies and those that were not grew wider.

Industrial archaeologists study the early history of our modern machine-based society. This is a vast subject. It includes the study of factories, the machines themselves and the goods they produced. It also covers everything connected with this, such as the houses specially built for factory workers and the water supplies both they and the factories needed.

The docks, railroads, canals, and locks used in carrying raw materials and finished products are also important, as are the warehouses, mining, and smelting equipment, and even the clothing used by workers and the toys or ornaments they made from scrap. The archaeologist working in this field must have a firm understanding of the principles of engineering and, in some cases, of chemistry, mining geology and other subjects connected with industry.

Industrial archaeology is centered in northwestern Europe and North America. Here inventions were produced and used in the eighteenth and nineteenth centuries. The spinning jenny revolutionized cotton spinning in Lancashire, England. Railroads spread across the United States, linking east and west, only a few decades after pioneers had traveled the same ground in covered wagons.

The industrial archaeologist has several tasks. The first is to discover and record as much as possible about how things were produced. Working closely with historians, the archaeologist can use contemporary accounts of factories or railroads, and may even succeed in finding original blueprints, patent

Steam locomotive, USA, 1870.

The world's first iron bridge, built to span the Severn River at Ironbridge, Shropshire, England, between 1777 and 1779.

The increasingly sophisticated use of water power was one of the most important elements of the Industrial Revolution. This tilt forge in Sheffield, England, was built in 1787 to make agricultural equipment. All the machinery is still in working order.

drawings, or a firm's own records. Nevertheless, many questions can only be answered by fieldwork. Sometimes no excavation is needed. The steam engine, factory, crane, or pump which interests the archaeologist may still be standing, even if in a neglected state. Here the task is to study and record, using photography to produce technical drawings. At other times it is necessary to dig. For example, at Saugus in Massachusetts, archaeologists excavated the seventeenth century village ironworks and smithy. Not only buildings were revealed but also details such as what fuel was used and how waste was dumped.

Industrial science moves forward quickly. Equipment is often destroyed once it has been replaced by more efficient machinery. Factory buildings are knocked down to make way for bigger ones. Canals are allowed to silt up and old machines are smashed for scrap. The industrial archaeologist must find and preserve these valuable examples of industrial history. Sometimes this requires a great deal of effort. The world's first iron-hulled steamship, the SS *Great Britain*, was recently rescued from a beach in the Falkland Islands where she had been rusting for many years. She was towed back to England to be restored and used as a floating museum.

One of the best ways of interesting the public and getting support for industrial archaeology is to restore machinery to working order and allow visitors to see it in action. Steam engines, pumping stations, early cars, streetcars, trains, and aircraft all attract visitors. They become aware of the value in finding and preserving other examples before they are lost forever to future generations.

Rescue Archaeology

In the last two centuries we have become more and more aware of our past. We have developed better and better ways to recover knowledge of it. At the same time, however, we have created new and more efficient ways to destroy it. This has led to the development of rescue archaeology, which sets out to salvage archaeological evidence threatened by immediate destruction.

The Industrial Revolution triggered off great social, political, and technical change in Europe and North America. In the present century this has spread over most of the world. We can alter the face of large areas of our planet in a way which would have been impossible only twenty or thirty years ago. This has led to widespread destruction of archaeological sites.

The range of this threat is enormous. New dams, new roads, large-scale mining, the expansion of cities and towns, and the bringing of virgin land under the plow change the natural environment. The uppermost layers of soil are moved and covered and it is just there that most archaeological remains are to be found. In some cases, such as the building of the Aswan High Dam in Egypt, or the creation of one of the world's largest artificial lakes, by damming the Volta River in Ghana, vast areas of land are submerged forever. These contain not only present-day towns and villages, but also the remains of many earlier ones. In other cases new buildings in ancient settlements, such as London or Athens, may need to have deep foundations which cut directly through important archaeological remains. Every time a pipeline is laid or a road built evidence of the past may be wiped out.

Rescue archaeology has developed to save as much of the past as possible in these circumstances. One of the aims of rescue archaeology is to make people aware of the dangers to their cultural heritage which exist today. In the USA, Britain, and many other countries, this is done by setting up local archaeological organizations and by encouraging young people to become interested in archaeology. These amateur archaeologists can then keep alert to any threats to archaeological sites and campaign to preserve them. Many countries have now passed laws to protect major archaeological remains from destruction.

The organizations must be provided with money to carry out excavations quickly and efficiently, before a site is bulldozed, drowned or buried forever. This may involve a major international operation such as that mounted at the temples of Abu Simbel in Egypt. There, buildings were taken to pieces and reconstructed above the new water level of the Aswan High Dam. Or it may mean simply providing a few skilled professional archaeologists to direct a larger group of volunteer amateurs to survey and, if necessary, excavate sites under immediate threat. Also excavated material has to be properly stored, studied, and an analysis published. Sometimes the companies and authorities involved in developing these sites have been persuaded to exhibit material. In this way, local people have been made aware of the importance of archaeology.

Rescue archaeology very often means emergency excavation which is forced upon archaeologists. Some archaeologists would prefer to excavate only those sites which they believe will test their theories and help solve particular problems. They dislike having to dig simply because a site is soon to be obliterated. Sometimes there is only time to dig a portion of a site rather than recover everything. Nevertheless, if rescue excavations are not carried out, unique evidence will be lost.

The lake created by the Aswan High Dam in Egypt threatened to submerge the famous temples of Abu Simbel, built by order of Pharaoh Ramses II between 1290 and 1223 BC. Engineers cut the huge sandstone temple into more than 1000 blocks which were then rebuilt on a higher site nearby.

Experiments in Archaeology

Archaeologists use experiments to check the conclusions they have reached from the evidence of their excavations. They also try to solve the problems that arise when the buried material they find has not been completely preserved. This is not a new idea, for in the last century scholars experimented with making flint tools, and in 1893 an exact copy of a Viking ship was test-sailed across the Atlantic. Since those days, many archaeologists have tried to reproduce methods of doing things that have been revealed by excavations. They have also tried to find out how objects might have been made and used. Such experiments are made frequently today; they are carried out on a large scale with great attention to detail.

Many experimental reconstructions have centered on food production. In Scandinavia and Britain, experimental farms have been set up where archaeologists have used and recorded the effects of, for example, slash and burn agriculture. Early farmers cut down trees and shrubs to clear a plot in the forest. They burned the vegetation and the ashes fertilized the soil. After several crops had been harvested, the soil became exhausted and yields became smaller. Then a new clearing was made and cultivated while the old one was allowed to grow back into the forest.

The experiments were interesting because they showed exactly how the pollen remains changed when this kind of agriculture was practiced. If pollen analysis from an excavation reveals a pattern which matches that of pollen from these experiments, archaeologists can be certain that the prehistoric farmers they are studying were using slash and burn methods.

Archaeologists have experimented with early types of plows drawn by oxen to see how efficient they were in breaking the ground and how long it took a farmer to plow his fields. Iron Age cattle have been created by breeding back from modern strains. They have also been butchered in the ways suggested by

One of the most exciting archaeological recreations is that at Trelleborg in Denmark, where an entire Viking settlement has been reconstructed following information from the sagas. The model opposite shows the layout of the whole village surrounded by its defensive walls and ditch. The houses (above and below) *have been built to resemble the houses which stood on the site when it was occupied around 1000 AD.*

bones found in archaeological sites. This showed how much meat was on the most popular joints and how many people they may have fed.

Experiments have been made into how food was stored. In Guatemala, tests on bottle-shaped pits lined with plaster have shown that they were used for water storage. A series of experiments showed that similar pits found in other parts of Central America were useless for water storage but excellent for the dry storage of the ramón nut. This was a very important source of food to the ancient Maya.

One kind of experimental reconstruction involves trying to build houses which would fit in with the pattern of ancient remains, for example postholes or stone foundations discovered by excavation. In several cases, these experiments have helped to show that earlier ideas on how they were built were wrong. The types of roofs or heights of walls that archaeologists had visualized would never have stayed up.

Experiments studying natural forces, such as erosion, which work on archaeological remains, may be said to go back to Charles Darwin. He studied how the activities of earthworms buried objects left on the surface of the ground. Worms take discarded soil to the surface and leave it there in casts. Modern archaeologists have built different types of earthworks and then observed how they settle, wear away, silt up, and are recolonized by plants. From this kind of experiment, they can work out how long earthwork fortifications were in use and how high the original earthbanks were. Attempts have been made to reproduce the conditions under which the stone in the walls of Scottish Iron Age forts became heated to temperatures so high that the rocks fused together. The fires that caused this may have been lit by the builders to produce particularly strong defensive walls.

The variety of present-day archaeological experiments is enormous. They range from navigating outrigger vessels on the Pacific Ocean to testing how efficient Bronze Age metal or leather shields were against swords and arrows. The leather shields proved the most efficient when the leather had been hardened in hot water and beaten into shape. The bronze ones were probably ornamental. Experiments are valuable because they reveal any shaky conclusions that have been reached by excavation alone and indicate points that should be examined in other excavations.

The Origins of Mankind

For how long have human beings walked the earth? When did they part company with their apelike ancestors? What did they inherit from them? Archaeologists do not yet have definite answers to these questions. However, in recent years they have made astonishing discoveries which suggest how these questions may eventually be answered.

Most of these discoveries have been made in East Africa, an area where early hominid fossil remains are preserved and easily reached. Many finds have been made by the Leakey family, Louis, his wife Mary and son Richard, excavating in the Olduvai Gorge in Tanzania and in Kenya. To the north, in the Afar region of Ethiopia, American archaeologists have also added to our knowledge of our early ancestors.

The evidence is slender. For the first three million or so years of our history, we have only a few boxes of fragmentary fossilized bones and some shaped stones. Yet from these scraps of skull, hand bones, pelvises, and other fragments we can begin to sketch the outlines of our own past.

The picture to emerge so far is like this. Possibly as much as four million years ago, creatures who could walk upright were living on the savanna of what is now Africa. This was far earlier than anyone had believed

likely until very recently. These creatures seem to have evolved from a type of ape called *Ramapithecus*, which flourished about ten to twelve million years ago. The hominid line branched off from this by about six million years ago. There seem to have been at least three distinct types of early hominid. Two of these, called *Australopithecus*, eventually disappeared. The third, *Homo habilis* ("handy man"), is thought to be one of our ancestors.

But when can we say "This is a human being"? Walking upright was an important stage in our evolution. It meant that the hands became free to carry, use, and eventually make things. A large brain was further evidence of development. But most significant were the signs that hominids were able to make things, shown at first by simple tools. These tools were roughly modified pebbles and stones. They have been found at Olduvai and in Ethiopia in association with hominid remains about one to two million years old. It is thought that *Homo habilis* made and used these.

The development of the human skull from the earliest Australopithecus fossil to modern man (homo sapiens sapiens).

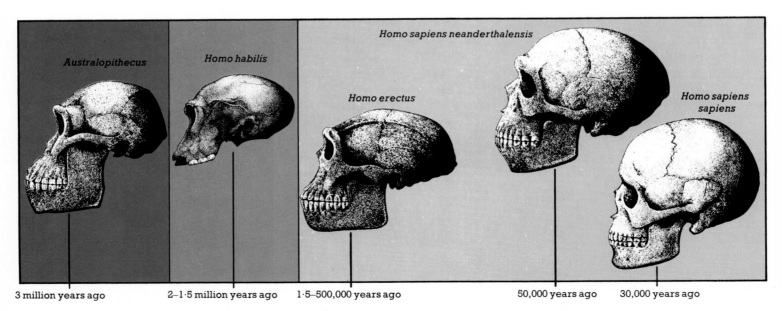

Australopithecus	Homo habilis	Homo erectus	Homo sapiens neanderthalensis	Homo sapiens sapiens
3 million years ago	2–1·5 million years ago	1·5–500,000 years ago	50,000 years ago	30,000 years ago

This skull of Peking Man, from Choukoutien, China, is between 600,000 and 300,000 years old.

Near Lake Eyasi, Tanzania, three footprints of early hominids have been found. Three individuals, possibly two adults and a child, walked across soft lakeside mud which became fossilized. Their footprints have given precious information about the development of mankind's upright posture.

As tool using continued, slowly becoming more sophisticated, other signs appeared which set our early ancestors apart from animals. Traces of fire, dating between 1 and 1.7 million years ago, have been found in China in Yunnan Province, and it was probably used by early *Homo erectus*. What is thought to be the earliest known building made by humans was found in East Africa. This is a two million year old circle of stones. Some of the stones were placed on top of others and these may have anchored the edges of a shelter made of branches.

About one million years ago in Africa a new form of tool began to appear which had many uses. It was the tear-drop shaped handax. This was probably invented by the gradually developing group of our ancestors known as *Homo erectus* ("upright man") which was soon to spread from tropical to temperate areas of the world. By about half a million years ago, it is clear from the remains of campsites that fire was under human control. The pace of human development began to accelerate. Peking Man, the name given to *Homo erectus* in China, may have practiced cannibalism. This is shown by the way human skulls were broken to extract the brains inside. Evidence from Spain indicates large group elephant hunts 300,000 years ago. By 50,000 years ago, Neanderthal people, probably our most recent ancestors, carefully buried their dead and sometimes covered the bodies with flowers.

There is still so much we do not know. We do not know when early people first began to speak or when they developed religious beliefs. Nevertheless, we can now see that our origins go back much farther than we ever thought possible.

The First Toolmakers

Front and side views of a chopper tool (below),
an early handax (center) and a
later, more carefully made, tear-drop
shaped handax (right).

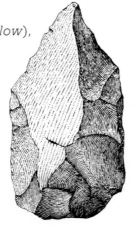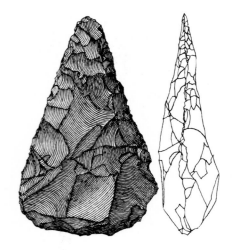

It used to be common to define the human species as the only animal that used tools. We now know that chimpanzees in their natural surroundings will poke sticks into termite mounds to get insects for eating. Earlier writers had pointed out that the Californian sea otter used stones to smash mollusk shells balanced on its chest as it floated on its back. Nevertheless, tool using still remains a standard by which to judge mankind. We belong to the only species which deliberately creates tools to a set pattern, rather than using natural objects. No other species uses tools to make other tools. We have now reached the point where we have machines to control machines which produce other machines for us! No other species is dependent on making and using tools for its survival.

The earliest implements which can be identified as tools come from East Africa, with some of the earliest hominid fossils. In the 1930s Louis and Mary Leakey found roughly chipped pebbles which they called chopper tools. He argued that these were the types of tools used before the well known stone hand-axes came into existence. In the early 1950s they found similar chopper tools in the lowest and earliest bed at Olduvai. In the 1960s new dating techniques, mainly the potassium-argon method, indicated that such tools were about two million years old. They were far older than anyone had considered possible. More recently, quartz tools have been found in the Omo valley, Ethiopia, which also have an age of two million years. Nobody knows for certain which early hominid group produced these. Many archaeologists favor *Homo habilis* as the tool user.

Nineteenth century archaeologists thought that the earliest tools would be crude in form. Many collections were made of eoliths, or "dawn stones," from the Pliocene epoch (five million years ago) and Miocene epoch (twenty-five million years ago). It

Wooden spear-tip found in the gravels at Clacton-on-Sea, Essex, England. It had been hardened in fire and is about 300,000 to 250,000 years old.

An experiment in Old Stone Age toolmaking at Hjerl Hede in Denmark. Schoolchildren spend their summer holidays at this reconstructed Old Stone Age village living and working as people of that time would have done.

was difficult to be sure if early people had fashioned these ancient stone tools. Natural crushing, sharp changes of temperature, and many other non-human forces can produce pebbles and rocks which look very similar to early chipped stone tools. For a tool to be accepted as an artifact, it must come from a period and a place which are recognized and dated. It must be one of a series of stones showing the same broad pattern of alteration. The many collections of eoliths are not now thought to be genuine. Leakey's collection, however, was quite clearly made up of tools rather than of products of natural action. The fact that they existed alongside the remains of extinct hominids raised the whole question of how and when human beings parted company from their apelike ancestors.

Primitive people may have scavenged the prey of wild animals. Once they began to kill large beasts themselves they would need weapons. The earliest wooden spear so far discovered dates only from about 300,000 to 250,000 years ago, but it is possible

that spears were in use far earlier. Early hunters would also need tools to cut up their kill, so hunting and tool using may well have gone together.

The chopper tools of the earliest period were gradually superceded by the handax, although the two co-existed for about half a million years. The axes seem to be the work of *Homo erectus*. We are still not certain how these handaxes were used. Certainly, they were used in hunting and cutting up game, as proved by finds of handaxes alongside the carcasses of large game animals. Most handaxes were chipped from a lump of stone. During the million year period in which they were made, their style and manufacture became more and more sophisticated. There is evidence of an increasing number of specialized tools made during the later part of the Old Stone Age (30,000–10,000 BC). By this time, the great variety of "tool-kits" shows how traditional methods of making tools were being adapted to suit the local conditions and local types of game. This is further evidence that people were able to exploit parts of their environment.

Hunters and Gatherers

Much of archaeology is the story of man the hunter and, usually, woman the gatherer. Agriculture and animal herding developed only recently, and even today several groups live in the ancient way, in remote areas of South America, Africa and Southeast Asia. A hundred years ago there were many more of these hunters, but they are now nearly all extinct, because of the encroachment of agricultural and industrial societies.

Our hominid ancestors probably lived on a mixed diet of vegetable matter and any insects and small creatures they could catch. The need to cooperate and plan when hunting larger animals may have pushed our early ancestors forward along the evolutionary path, because planning and cooperation require communication, which probably helped the development of speech. Peking Man, who lived about 500,000 years ago, was clearly a great hunter. Animal remains have been found at the Chinese site of Chou-koutien. Deer, leopard, cave-bear, saber-toothed tiger, hyena, elephant, horse, and boar were hunted. From the Mesolithic period we have the remains of fishnets and traps. Domestic rubbish heaps, called middens, have been found in some coastal areas. These tell us that some early groups relied on fish and shellfish for food and camped near their food supplies.

Most hunting and gathering peoples have definite patterns in their lives and usually divide the work. The men concentrate on catching and killing the larger animals, the women, children, and the elderly gather roots, berries, fruits, and insects and some-times fish and trap small game. Life also has a definite seasonal pattern. During part of the year, animal and plant food is abundant and large groups of people can gather together to hunt and feast. At other times, game is scarce and the people must split into groups and spread out, following the game as it searches for food.

Careful excavation of bison skeletons at a site in southeastern Colorado led to the discovery of ways in which Indian hunters butchered the animals 8500 years ago.

The archaeologist comes across several distinct kinds of site. There are those occupied by a few people during the season when game was scarce, and those occupied by larger groups when food was plentiful. There are also kill sites, places at which animals were killed. The first two kinds might be occupied year after year, and kill sites may be close to both kinds of camp. By examining the settlement sites, archaeologists can reconstruct the size of the group and discover details of their diet. By studying the plant and pollen evidence, they may also work out at which season the site was used. Excavations in the Zagros Mountains in Turkey have discovered residential base camps from which hunting parties made seasonal forays to more transitory settlements from which they hunted game. The meat was then cut

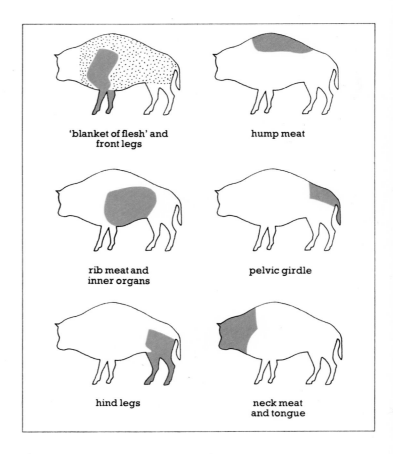

'blanket of flesh' and front legs

hump meat

rib meat and inner organs

pelvic girdle

hind legs

neck meat and tongue

Women of the Chenchu tribe, India, digging up edible roots.

Cave painting showing an Old Stone Age hunter attacked by a bison, Lascaux, France. The colors were made from minerals and plants.

up at temporary butchering stations, whose remains show that hoofed animals made up 90% of the catch. By studying such sites it is possible to work out the territory over which the hunting groups ranged.

A great deal can be learned from kill sites. They often give evidence of hunting methods, and the animal skeletons may contain broken or unrecovered weapons. The way the animals were butchered may tell us something about the size of the hunting band.

At a site in a dry ravine in southeastern Colorado, the remains of nearly two hundred bison have been excavated. They were slaughtered in about 6500 BC. The bones lay in three distinct layers. The whole corpses were at the bottom, slightly cut about corpses in the middle and then, at the top, the skeletons which had been dismembered. The bison had been stampeded into the ravine from the north. The first to fall in were trapped by those which crashed on top of them. The way the bones of the dismembered skeletons were piled indicated the order in which the topmost carcasses had been cut up. Judging from the work involved, the amount of meat produced and how long it would probably stay fresh, it was calculated that the group of hunters and their dependents consisted of about a hundred and fifty people. The remains of newborn calves were also found, which showed that the hunt had taken place in May or early June.

51

The First Farmers

Where game and wild plants were plentiful, people who lived by hunting and gathering were able to develop large permanent settlements like Lepenski Vir in Yugoslavia. Here the population relied heavily on fishing in the Danube. Villages and towns did not develop in most parts of the world until our ancestors changed from hunting and gathering to growing crops and tending animals. They became farmers.

Archaeologists once thought that this change to agriculture happened fairly suddenly. It led to a rapid increase in food production, population, and the growth of villages. This was known as the Neolithic Revolution. But there are now good reasons for believing that it was a slower, more subtle series of events which occurred at different times and in different parts of the world, and at different speeds in different regions. Farmers were growing wheat and barley about nine thousand years ago in the Zagros and Taurus Mountains of Mesopotamia and Anatolia (Turkey). But it was not until about four thousand years later that Scandinavian peoples first started growing crops.

Hunters and gatherers did not usually kill the wild animals and uproot the plants on which they depended in an uncontrolled way. They tended to concentrate on particular types and ages of animals or particular plant foods. Rarely did they threaten to wipe out the species. Some gatherers changed their surroundings by burning or clearing undergrowth, to help favorite kinds of plants to grow. Others evolved a way of life which was very dependent upon wild animals such as reindeer. As early farmers gradually bred wild plants and animals, the species changed. The main cause of this was the way they brought about genetic changes in the animals and plants to suit their own needs. In this way they made those species dependent on them. Domesticated

Egyptian wall painting from the Tomb of Menna, about 1425 BC. Menna is standing at the top left-hand corner supervising the work and the punishment of a slave (center). On the right of the bottom panel oxen are walking in the ears of grain to thresh it (separate the grain from the chaff). On the left a group of slaves toss the threshed grain into the air so that the light chaff blows away and the heavy grain falls to the ground to be collected and stored for use.

emmer wheat

einkorn wheat

bread wheat

wild wheat

later domesticated varieties

These drawings show stages in the domestication of wheat. Wild types with small seeds were gradually selectively bred to produce varieties with much bigger grains.

This map shows the areas of early agriculture in the Near East. Surprisingly, they are all in dry areas, where food plants did not grow naturally in particularly great abundance. The wild ancestors of wheat, barley and beans were, however, found in these areas, as were sheep, goats, and cattle. People living under harsh conditions had to develop methods to guarantee their food supply, and so began plant cultivation and animal domestication.

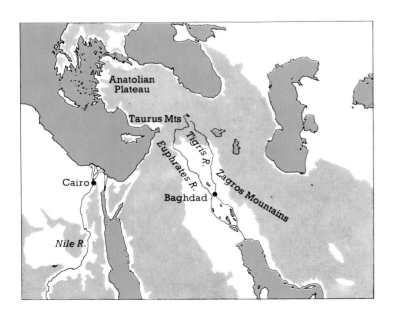

animals were separated from the wild animals to avoid interbreeding. Plants were grown in places where particular varieties could thrive and cross-breed through proximity. In this way new strains were produced which would ripen within a short period and were convenient for people to harvest. The early farmers used animals increasingly. Draft animals pulled plows and carts and goats and sheep provided milk and wool. This was possible because the farmers looked after their animals, giving them food and shelter.

The first steps in cultivating plants seem to have been taken in areas which were on the borders of, and not in, the fertile alluvial valleys of the Tigris and Euphrates Rivers of Mesopotamia. The Zagros and Taurus Mountains, the basins of the Anatolian Plateau, and the high, arid basin around the Tehuacán valley, Mexico, contain sites with evidence of the earliest cultivation of cereals. Conditions here were difficult and so the early settlers, forced by pressure of population growth from the good land, probably had to deliberately develop and foster local food supplies.

Agriculture was well under way by 5000 BC in many areas scattered throughout Anatolia and Mesopotamia and in Mexico, maize cultivation began at about the same period, but it took a longer time before cultivated plants were more important in the diet than gathered food. The breeding of plants, such as rice, yam, and sweet potato, happened independently in other areas such as China, western Asia, and Africa. Agriculture was being practiced 5000 BC or earlier in the highlands of New Guinea, where taro, a starchy root, was being grown.

If we study how modern crops originated and developed, and where the related wild species occur, we can work out where they may first have been cultivated. It is far more difficult to interpret animal bones to tell if they are from wild or domesticated species. But the proportion of certain ages or sexes of animals in the archaeological record may show that early farmers had started to breed and maintain the type of herd they preferred. There is evidence that people living in Anatolia and Mesopotamia had domesticated animals such as dogs, goats, sheep and cattle by 5000 BC.

The Origins of Cities

The first cities grew up about 5500 years ago. They had populations of only a few thousand and served as administrative, trading, and religious centers which were in direct contact with the surrounding farmland. City life of the type we know today began only 100–150 years ago, during the Industrial Revolution, when people migrated from the countryside to the new industrial and manufacturing centers.

The world's earliest cities grew from villages in Mesopotamia and in the Nile valley of Egypt about 3500–3000 BC. A thousand years later, cities appeared in the Indus valley of Pakistan, and by 1500 BC cities were built near the Yellow River in China. These cities developed because of the annual flooding of the great rivers, which fertilized the land and made it possible to grow large crops of grain every year. Later, between 500 and 100 BC, the first cities were built in Central America. Similar conditions seem to have encouraged these centers of great civilizations to grow. Farming methods had to be efficient so that a surplus of food could be built up to feed larger numbers of people. When this happened not everyone

needed to work on the land. Some people began to specialize in crafts such as pottery and jewelry making. Many early civilizations used bronze tools, plowed their fields, and used the wheel in transport and machinery. In all the early known civilizations writing was an important part of city life. Accounts and inventories could be kept, laws, and religious teachings written down. As some people learned to write and the work load was distributed, a ruling class developed. This group usually controlled both civil government and religious power. This aristocracy, once established, could organize the huge teams of laborers needed in large scale construction work, such as building fortifications, irrigation systems, temples, and palaces.

The great Indus civilization, which flourished in India and Pakistan about 2300 to 1750 BC, dominated the plains of the Indus River and its tributaries. Wheat and barley were the main crops grown to feed the citizens of Harappa and Mohenjo-Daro, the twin capital cities, about 400 miles apart. Life in these early cities was highly organized. The cities themselves

Some of the earliest known cities.

This stern-faced stone statue of a priest-king was found in the citadel of Mohenjo-Daro.

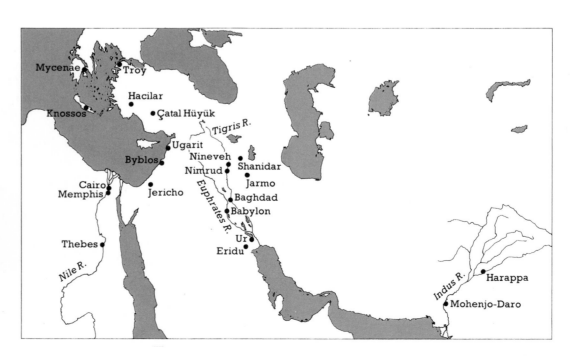

54

The citadel at Mohenjo-Daro rises about forty-five feet to the west of the city's residential area.

were also carefully planned. They were divided into an upper citadel and a lower residential area. The citadels were fortresses used for defensive and religious purposes. They also contained huge granaries complete with ventilation systems to prevent the stored grain from rotting. At Harappa, the ruined mud-brick walls, thirty-nine feet thick, still stand to a height of forty-nine feet, protecting the city's heart.

At Mohenjo-Daro, excavations in the citadel re-vealed a large bath like a swimming-pool and a spacious assembly hall. East of the citadel lay the residential part of the city. Houses, which varied in size from many-roomed mansions to one-roomed apartments, were laid out in a grid pattern. Homes were built of standard-sized mud bricks with wooden roofs and had blank windowless walls facing the main street. Entrances and windows were in side streets and courtyards. The paved streets were kept very clean. Nearly every house had a special bathroom which was linked to an elaborate drainage system.

The mysterious Indus script has still to be de-ciphered. Inscriptions in this language have been found on many seals and seal impressions. They were probably used to secure bales of merchandise and bore the name of the owner. Uniform weights and measures were in use. Long-distance trade between the cities of the Indus civilization and ancient Meso-potamia was well established. Trade contacts reached far to the east and west for precious stones, north to Afghanistan for silver and south to Mysore for gold. Within the Indus area bronze, iron, and stone tools were designed to regular patterns, and styles in pot-tery, jewelry and seal motifs are remarkably similar throughout the whole area.

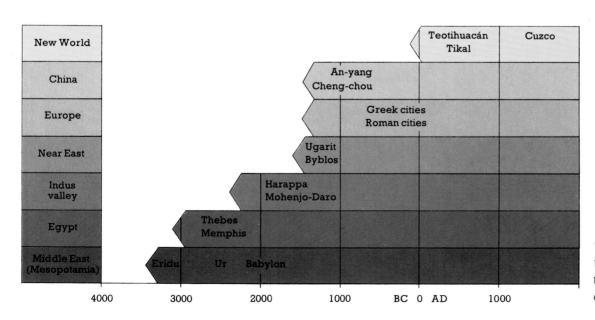

	4000	3000	2000	1000	BC 0 AD	1000	
New World						Teotihuacán Tikal	Cuzco
China				An-yang Cheng-chou			
Europe					Greek cities Roman cities		
Near East				Ugarit Byblos			
Indus valley			Harappa Mohenjo-Daro				
Egypt		Thebes Memphis					
Middle East (Mesopotamia)	Eridu	Ur Babylon					

This time-chart shows where and when the world's first great civilizations developed.

55

Writing and its Decoding

Writing was invented about 3500 BC in Mesopotamia. In its earliest form it was no more than drawings of the things referred to (pictograms). However, it soon developed to represent ideas (ideograms) and then, most importantly, to record the sounds of speech. The effects were profound. Until this point, knowledge could be passed on only by direct example and by word of mouth. Now it could be stored and passed on to people many miles or generations apart.

Writing can therefore help us to understand the ideas and thoughts of people who died long before we were born. But first we must be able to read what they wrote, and for many years scholars have struggled to decipher the scripts of long-dead civilizations.

To decipher an unknown script, we must first know or guess the language the writer was using. We must also obtain as many texts in that script and language as possible. We will then have a body of material to work on and to test our interpretations. Finally, we must link the signs and symbols used to sounds, words, phrases, and meanings in that language and discover the language's grammar.

Reading an unknown language is much easier if the same text can be found written in a known language. It was just such a discovery which led to the decipherment of Egyptian hieroglyphics, the picture-like writing of the ancient Egyptian priests. In 1799 Napoleon's troops discovered, at Rosetta in Egypt, a stone on which there was an inscription in three scripts. One was Greek, the others ancient Egyptian scripts, one hieroglyphic and the other a cursive, or flowing, form of vernacular writing known as demotic. It was soon realized that the same passage might be written in each language.

An English scholar, Thomas Young, noted that some of the hieroglyphs enclosed in oval frames (cartouches) represented the name of the king, Ptolemy, in the readable Greek text. A young French scholar, Jean François Champollion, worked on from there. He established that there were three times as many signs in the hieroglyphic text as in the Greek text. Each hieroglyph, therefore, could not represent a single word, for there would be more words in one text than the other. He then worked out the phonetic or sound value for the names in the cartouches, aided by his realization that the demotic and hieroglyphic scripts had both been used to write an early form of Coptic. This was the language of Christian Egyptians spoken about 500–700 AD. This gave him many clues to the structure of words and their sounds, and soon he had cracked the code. In 1824 he published his findings. The way was clear for a greater understanding of Ancient Egypt.

The decoding of ancient cuneiform inscriptions from Assyria was also helped by the discovery of the same text in different languages. There is a huge triple inscription on the sheer face of a cliff in Iran, the Behistun Rock. The inscription was put there in 516 BC at the order of Darius I, King of Persia, to proclaim his victories. The text is in Elamite, Old Persian and

The development of Mesopotamian cuneiform. Pictograms, the earliest type of writing, represented only what was drawn. As the symbols became stylized into cuneiform, they acquired abstract meanings (ideograms). Ancient Egyptian hieroglyphs developed in a similar way.

	Pictograms			Cuneiform				Meaning
	3500 BC	3100 BC	2800 BC	2400BC Sumerian		1700 BC Babylonian	700 BC Assyrian	
								head/front
								bird

The Rosetta Stone. The upper inscription is in hieroglyphic characters, the middle in demotic and the lower in Greek.
The name of the Egyptian Pharaoh, Ptolemy, written in hieroglyphs which represent the syllables of his name. The oval cartouche around the hieroglyphs gave magical protection. Ptolemy's name was found on the Rosetta Stone.

Babylonian, Henry Rawlinson, an English diplomat, copied it in the 1830s and 1840s. He found a key to help unlock the code in the favorite Persian royal title of ''King of Kings.'' There was a recurring phrase in the inscription which seemed to fit this. Gradually, he was able to read and translate the Old Persian text and then the other texts.

The most famous decipherment of recent years is that of Linear B. This is a syllabic script, first found in 1900 on clay tablets from Knossos in Crete and dating from the thirteenth century BC. In 1952 it was discovered that the language used was an early form of Greek. The inscribed clay tablets finally proved to be mainly stocktaking lists and inventories!

There are still scripts that await decipherment, such as Linear A from Crete which was used from about 1700 to 1600 BC, but it may be a computer that will unlock these doors to the past.

Pottery and the Wheel

Pottery making and the discovery of the wheel are among the most important human inventions. The wheel became the basis of the countless rotary machines, with parts turning on an axis, without which our present society would come to a virtual standstill.

The first baked clay objects so far discovered date from about 25,000 BC. Stone Age artists had discovered that figurines (small statuettes) modeled in easily worked clay would harden when placed near a fire. The first known pottery vessels come from Japan and date from around 10,000 BC. At Mureybet in Syria, pots were made in about 8000 BC and about 7500 BC at Ganjdareh, Iran. Exactly where and when pottery was first invented has still to be discovered. But by 6000 BC there was widespread use of hand-made pottery in the Zagros region of Iraq. By 4000 BC specialist potters were beginning to appear.

The pottery of this early period shows great technical skill and is often beautifully decorated. Most of it was made by methods still in use in many parts of the world. It was built up by smoothing together long coils of clay, or pulled up from a large lump, or made by joining rolled out sheets of clay. By 5000 BC a two-chambered kiln had been invented, which separated the pots from the fire that was to bake them. This was a great improvement on the bonfire where the pots were simply placed in a pit beneath an open fire. By 4000 BC pots were being spun on a slow, hand- or foot-turned, turntable. A thousand years later the fast wheel had been invented. This was a wheel, perhaps with a lower fly wheel, which was kept spinning, so that the speed at which the lump of clay turned helped to shape its form. It was very much like a modern potter's wheel. This led to pottery being made to a set pattern and being mass produced.

The invention and spread of pottery helped early people when they settled in one place and lived in villages. It allowed them to store liquids and grain and replace the earlier sorts of wooden, hide, bas-

Painted pot from the Nazca valley, Peru, made in about the sixth century AD. The human figure is flanked by two trophy heads, and wears a tunic decorated with stylized animal heads.

The earliest pottery yet found, from Fukui, Japan, dated about 10,000 BC.

An Assyrian cylinder seal with a cuneiform inscription and a scene from a lion hunt. The huntsman stands in a light chariot with two spoked wheels.

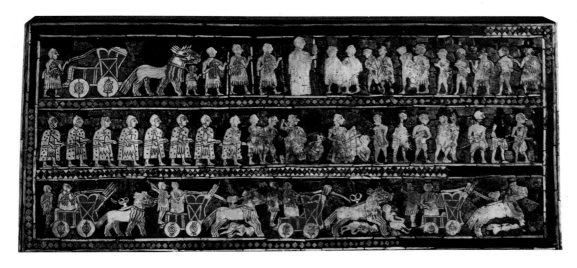

The Royal Standard of Ur, dated at about 2750 BC, shows chariots with solid wheels pulled into battle by teams of four asses.

ketry, or gourd vessels. Pottery seems to have been developed at different times in different parts of the world. The first American pottery is dated to about 3000 BC and pottery was in use in China by about 4500 BC.

In the West we associate the wheel with transport. As early as 3500 BC wheeled vehicles were in use in Sumer (the earliest civilization in southern Mesopotamia) for transport and warfare. It is possible that wheels evolved from tree trunks used as rollers to shift heavy weights. Early wheeled vehicles seem to have developed after sledges, which were well suited to the sandy summers and muddy winters of Sumer. The earliest wheels discovered were solid disks made of three pieces of wood. Examples of wagons using such wheels were excavated at Ur and date from about 3000 BC. Remains of skeletons show that these were pulled by oxen and onagers. Sometime between 2000 and 1500 BC two revolutionary things happened. The spoked wheel was invented which was lighter and stronger but much more difficult to make. Also horses began to be used to pull wheeled vehicles. For many hundreds of years after this the chariot was important in warfare.

Although the history of the West is closely involved with the use of the wheel, it was not known or used until recently in many areas. In America, although wheeled toys were made, humans or pack animals carried everything that had to be moved. But after the horse was introduced by Europeans, goods were dragged behind. In Africa, wheeled vehicles were used in the Sahara in about 300 AD but their use died out and the wheel was not used south of the Sahara until European colonization.

The Copper Age

The use of metal, like the spread of farming and pottery, appeared in different parts of the world at different times. Copper was the first metal to be used for making tools after stone, though in the old Three Age System, the Bronze Age was supposed to follow on directly after the New Stone Age. The Copper Age, or Chalcolithic, is the name used for the period of European prehistory from 7000 to 2000 BC. It was a time when flaked and polished stone was still the normal material for tools, but copper was used to make ornamental objects and ceremonial weapons.

At the ancient site of Cayönü Tepesi in Anatolia (modern Turkey), nuggets of native copper were cold-hammered into shape to make tools at about 7200 BC. Later it was discovered that native copper and copper ores could be melted and poured into molds to make more complicated shapes. The smelting of ores and casting of metal (metallurgy) represent a great advance in prehistoric technology. Copper metallurgy was known in Mesopotamia from about 4000 BC. Copper smelting developed at Çatal Hüyük, in Anatolia, before 5000 BC. Archaeological finds of copper axes in southeastern Europe and large urban settlements such as Karanovo in Bulgaria suggest that copper working was well-established in the Balkans by 4000 BC. Metal prospectors and traders explored the rich copper sources of the Carpathian and Slovakian mountains.

The Beaker People of western Europe seem to be the latest group belonging to the Copper Age. Between 2300 BC and 1700 BC they migrated and settled over much of Europe from Iberia (modern Spain and Portugal) east as far as Poland and north to the British Isles. They introduced the use of copper into Britain and put pottery beakers in the graves of their dead. People often put grave goods, such as jewelry, food, drink, money, and clothing, into graves to equip the dead person for the afterlife. The Beaker people buried beautifully made flint arrowheads and archers' wrist guards made of stone, gold earrings and copper pins, and knives with their dead. In England, they were responsible for building the huge circular monument at Avebury.

In the Americas, the earliest known metalwork in both continents belongs to the "Old Copper" people. They flourished from 4000 to 2000 BC in the area of the Great Lakes around Michigan, Wisconsin, and Ontario. The Old Copper metalworkers never discovered how to smelt ores or cast molten copper.

hearths
mud and timber walls
trench with palisade
post holes

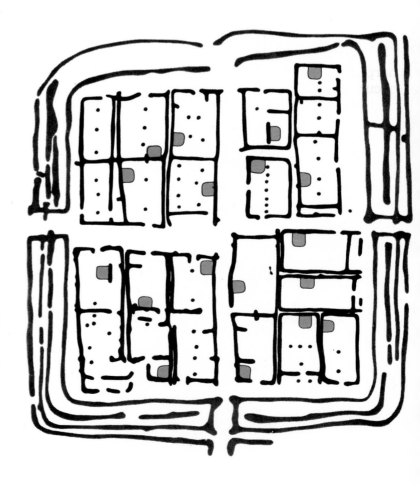

Plan of Copper Age village at Polyanista, Bulgaria, which existed about 4500 BC.

Two examples of beaten-copper work made by craftsmen of the Hopewell Indian culture. Left is a raven or crow in flight and above is a stylized double-headed eagle.

Instead they hammered out knives, chisels, axes, harpoon heads, and projectile points from naturally occurring lumps of copper. These tools are copies of earlier models made in other materials such as stone, bone, horn, and shell. The main advance in this age was the method of making of points and sockets for spearheads. The flattened copper was rolled around wood or stone to give it shape, so fixing it more firmly on to the shafts of weapons.

Much later, in about 200 AD, the coppersmiths of the Hopewell culture, in Ohio, produced hammered-out copper sheet. They cut this to shape and decorated it with intricate designs pushed from the back so they stood out in relief. They made bird and snake effigies, rings, ear ornaments, breastplates, and headdresses, and even large ax blades. Most of what is known about the Hopewell people comes from grave goods found in large burial mounds. There are many exotic treasures such as conch shells from the Gulf of Mexico, obsidian blades from the Southwest or the Rockies, canine teeth from grizzly bears, inlaid with freshwater pearls, and mysterious hand shapes cut from sheets of mica brought from Virginia. The villages of this artistic people were built in the fertile valleys where they grew wheat and hunted and gathered.

A Beaker burial from Shrewton, in Wiltshire, England, complete with a typical Beaker pot and flaked flint knife.

The Bronze Age

Bronze is a deliberate mixture of the metals copper and tin which produces a combination, or alloy, which is far stronger than either of its parts. Bronze is much tougher than copper and edged tools and weapons made of bronze stay sharper longer than those made of copper. Ten per cent tin to 90 per cent copper was discovered to be the ideal alloy, although early bronzesmiths often had to make do with far less tin. It is rare and difficult to extract with primitive mining and panning techniques.

The major sources of tin in prehistoric Europe were Cornwall (England), northwest Iberia (Spain), Bohemia, and Hungary. The biggest copper-bearing deposits were in central Europe. Mineral prospectors from the towns of Anatolia and Mesopotamia, which had been using bronze since about 3000 BC, traveled across Europe looking for ores. One of the most important results of the development of metal-using

Chinese bronze ritual wine vessel excavated in Honan province in 1955. It was made during the Shang dynasty – sixteenth to fifteenth centuries BC.

Reconstruction drawing of the type of tomb in which people of the central European Unĕtice culture often buried their dead. The wooden tomb chamber was covered with a mound or barrow.

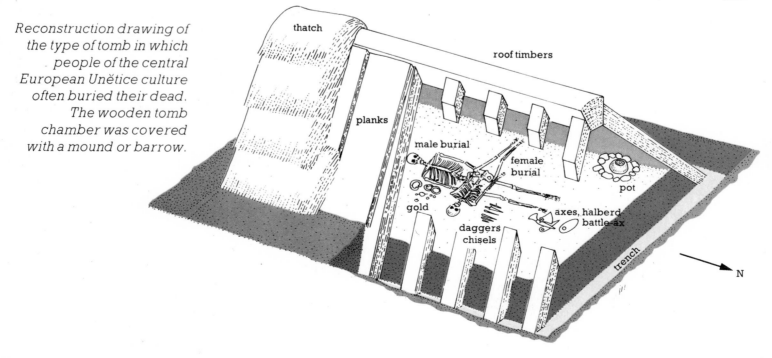

thatch

roof timbers

planks

male burial

female burial

pot

gold

axes, halberd battle-ax

daggers chisels

trench

N

Bronze Age harp player from the Greek island of Amorgos, dated 2400 to 2200 BC.

was covered by a massive timber mortuary house, which was then thatched. That in turn was covered by large stones and earth to make a high tumulus or mound. Centered in Czechoslovakia, the people of the Unětice culture mined the rich copper veins in Transylvania and are famous for their beautifully made bronze daggers and metal-shafted halberds. These have been found in places as far away as Denmark and Britain. Trading links with distant Egypt and the Aegean are shown by colorful ceramic beads, made of a blue-green glass-like substance, found in Unětice graves.

At the same time, Bronze Age civilizations flourished in the Aegean. The people of Troy, Mycenae, and Crete lived in stone-walled towns, used chariots in warfare and produced great works of art. They represent the beginnings of the great civilizations of ancient Greece and Rome, yet still shared many of the traits of their barbarian neighbors in central and northern Europe. They had close ties with these peoples whom they contacted in the course of trade. The close contact between the Mycenaean and the rich and powerful Wessex people in Britain is shown by the find of nearly identical bone-inlaid scepters in the Bush Barrow burial of a Wessex chieftain in Wiltshire and in one of the royal graves at Mycenae itself.

New lands were opened up, for bronze axes were suitable for clearing woodland. Bronze weapons helped in the conquest of less developed peoples. Rapiers and other long-handled thrusting weapons were a great improvement on the Wessex and Unětice daggers. Slashing swords with cutting edges on each side of the blade were invented. The Bronze Age was a period of great change throughout Europe.

civilizations was that a trade in raw materials and finished objects was created. This produced a network of routes by sea, river, and land. It also led to the development of a class of middlemen, local chiefs who gained control of and organized the supply and exchange of raw materials and exotic products. These middlemen became very powerful and wealthy. Most of the archaeological information about the Bronze Age comes from the burials of such aristocrats and from the bronze objects themselves.

In central Europe, for example, rich burials of the Unětice culture of 2000 to 1600 BC have been excavated, to show how the dead chieftain was buried lying down with a woman, perhaps a sacrificed wife, stretched across his lap. Surrounding him were golden necklets, pins, and precious jewelry. He was also supplied with bronze daggers, chisels, axes, and halberds (long-handled battleaxes). The grave

The Iron Age

Reconstruction of a circular Iron Age hut (500 BC–1 BC), Avoncroft, England.

The great Hittite civilization of central Anatolia kept secret its skills of iron ore smelting and iron-working for a long time. From about 1500 to 1200 BC the Hittites had exclusive control over iron tools and weapons. Then their empire collapsed under attack in about 1200 BC and their secret knowledge spread. Iron was a great improvement on bronze, especially for weapons, because of its strength. By about 1000 BC iron was commonly used for tools in Greece and Italy. By the seventh and sixth centuries BC the technique of ironworking was known in Europe and China. It was put to practical use while decorative work, including metal vessels and personal ornaments, were still made in bronze. This could be cast, hammered, and inlaid easily. Ironworking technology was confined to the heating and hammering techniques of the blacksmith.

Widespread demand for iron spearheads, swords, axes, and hoes led to the development of the ore deposits in Austria, southern Germany and Iberia. The warrior chiefs of these areas traded these raw materials to the Mediterranean city states. In return, they received luxury goods, such as classical bronze wine-mixing vessels, Greek painted pottery, bronze cauldrons on tripods, and jars full of wine. So trading centers developed in northern and central Europe, such as the towns of Heuneberg and

Manching, in Germany. On the shores of the Mediterranean, the Phoenicians set up colonies at Carthage (in Tunisia) and Tartessos (in Spain). The Greeks founded Marseilles and built ports in Sicily.

The Celtic craftsmen of Iron Age Europe produced quite superb metalwork. Classical designs were adapted and changed into flowing abstract and zoomorphic (animal) designs. The two main periods of the Iron Age are known as the Hallstatt (700–450 BC) and the La Tène (450–55 BC), both based on changes in artistic style in metal working. Because Britain was not occupied by the Romans until 43 AD, artistic development in style continued longer than in other parts of Europe. In Ireland, the Iron Age lasted until about 1000 AD, where deeds of warrior chiefs were being written down by Celtic Christian monks.

It was not until much later that European blacksmiths developed the means to cast iron. This involves melting the metal completely and pouring it into a mold. In China, however, cast ironwork came before the discovery of hammering methods or wrought ironwork. In the seventh century BC farming tools were skilfully cast, entailing the use of temperatures of at least 3360°F. The high temperatures were probably possible because of the early development of very efficient pottery kilns, constructed

Above: Bronze bucket found in an Iron Age cemetery at Hallstatt, Austria. The bucket, which stands 12 inches high, was made in about 600 BC.

Left: A Greek bronze vessel, 5 feet 4 inches tall, used for mixing wine. It was found in the grave of a Celtic Iron Age princess buried around 500 BC at Vix, France.

to fire porcelain. Wrought ironwork was only developed centuries later under the Han dynasty of 206 BC to 220 AD.

Africa passed directly from the Stone Age to the Iron Age. The Kingdom of Meroë in the Sudan, which flourished from 395 BC to 350 AD, was the center of early ironsmelting on the Nile. It probably derived its technology from Egypt.

Ironworking techniques probably reached West Africa from trading contacts with the North African coast. The people of the Nok culture in Nigeria were smelting and working iron by the third century BC. In East Africa, two streams of people who used iron gradually migrated south, east, and west from the earliest Iron Age settlements of 300 BC around Lake Victoria. During the eleventh century AD, there was a rapid spread of peoples who worked and used iron, in Africa south of the Equator. As a result, several stone-walled trading centers with impressive architecture were built, such as Great Zimbabwe in Zimbabwe. Its labyrinthine walls surrounded a commercial and religious center with far reaching connections.

The walls of Great Zimbabwe, in modern Zimbabwe, were built around 800 to 1500 AD to protect one of southern Africa's most important trading centers.

65

Transport by Land and Sea

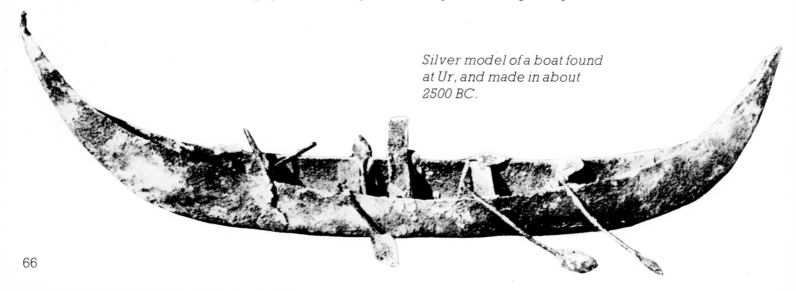

In the past three million years human beings have reached and populated most corners of the earth. They have developed ways of life which allow them to live in the snow and ice of Arctic winters and in the hot, sandy deserts of the Kalahari. Most traveling has been done on foot. Sometimes it was over temporary land bridges that emerged during the glacial periods in the last Ice Age when the level of the sea fell. It was in this way, perhaps as long ago as 40,000 BC, that the first inhabitants of the Americas arrived in Alaska. They traveled from northern Asia across the land bridge which spanned the Bering Straits.

In some parts of the world, particularly in America before European colonization, most loads were carried by men and women. They used tumplines, or straps which run across the forehead or upper chest, attached to bundles or baskets which they carried on their backs. The use of wheels and pack animals was unknown to them. In Mesopotamia, domesticated oxen drew two- and four-wheeled carts and wagons in 3500 BC. Chariots with spoked wheels were drawn by horses in Anatolia two thousand years later. In the far North, in 2000 BC, Arctic hunters were following their prey on skis, transporting tents and domestic equipment on large

Rock carving showing prehistoric travelers in Scandinavia using early skis or snowshoes.

sledges pulled by dogs.

We do not know when people first took to the water. But those living near rivers and lakes may have known how to swim and used logs or inflated animal skins to float on. Only a very few early boats have been found and excavated. A dugout, dated by the carbon 14 method to 6400 BC, was found at Pesse in The Netherlands. It had been made by hollowing out a tree trunk.

Paintings and engravings sometimes show boats, but they are often too simplified to tell the archaeologist much about their construction. Some pictures, however, such as wallpaintings in Egyptian tombs, give much detailed information. At about 3000 BC Egyptian boats were made of bundles of papyrus reeds tied together and paddled along. By 2500 BC the Egyptians were building seaworthy wooden ships with single, square sails. Rafts were used to

Silver model of a boat found at Ur, and made in about 2500 BC.

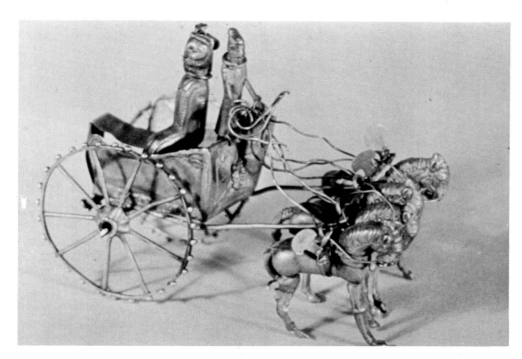

Gold model of a Persian war-chariot, made in about 500 BC.

ferry large, heavy loads such as huge stone blocks used in building temples and pyramids. In Scandinavia, rock engravings show small kayaks, rather like canoes, and oval coracles made from animal skins stretched over wooden frames. Large boats, powered by as many as thirty oars, were sailing on the Mediterranean by 2500 BC and similar vessels are shown on Danish carvings a thousand years later.

There are other parts of the world, such as the islands of the Pacific Ocean, which could not have been reached without the use of seagoing craft and considerable navigational skill.

In order to discover how early craft were navigated, exciting experiments have been carried out. Thor Heyerdahl, the Norwegian anthropologist, sailed the balsa-log raft *Kon Tiki* from the mainland of South America to Polynesia in the South Pacific. This was to prove such a voyage was possible. The cultivation of sweet potatoes and the presence of similar words in the languages of the two areas had hinted at long-distance sea contact at an early date. In 1978 a leather boat was made according to descriptions in medieval documents. It was sailed across the Atlantic from Ireland to North America to show that the legend that the Celtic St. Brendan had discovered America in the sixth century might be true.

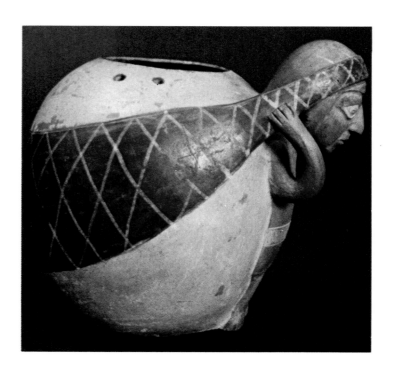

The Moche culture of Peru is noted for its fine ceramics. This bowl, showing an Indian using a tumpline to carry a load, was made between 200 and 700 AD.

Evidence from Coins

Silver tetradrachm (four drachma piece) from Athens, minted in 440–430 BC.

Coins make the exchange of goods and services easier. They help us to place a common set of values on a wide range of different things. They obviously aid the growth of urban and trading societies. Their first known use was about 630 BC in Lydia in Turkey. Ever since then, people have been using them, and coins turn up in archaeological excavations. Sometimes they were lost accidentally. They fell from purses or pockets while people were in markets, walking down streets, or fording streams. At other times hoards of coins were hidden to keep them safe in times of trouble and the owners never returned to find them. Occasionally, however, they were buried for a different reason. The great Anglo-Saxon ship burial at Sutton Hoo contained a purse holding thirty-seven small gold coins, three circular blanks and two small bars of gold. Perhaps these were placed there to pay each member of the ghostly crew of the ship!

Coins are struck or cast from metal, often gold or silver. This has helped to preserve them if they are buried in the earth, because these metals do not corrode easily. In the earliest days of coinage, each Greek city issued its own coins, usually marked on one side with an emblem symbolizing the gods who protected the city, such as the owl for Athena and Athens. At a later period, rulers began to place their portraits, the dates of minting and claims to power on coins, a practice continued to the present day.

Finds of coins are valuable to the archaeologist in

Copper ingot probably used as currency in Zambia, in southern-central Africa, in the fourteenth century AD.

In the third century BC, the Celtic tribes of northwestern Europe began to copy the gold coinage of Macedonia, shown at the top. Gradually, as the Celtic coins, middle and bottom, show, the classical design of a portrait head and horse-drawn chariot became stylized until they were quite unrecognizable.

Analysis of the metal in coins can also indicate something of the political conditions under which they were made. Coins which have been made from a mixture of gold or silver with less precious metals show a weak economy and possibly weak rulers. On the other hand, the fact that coinage of pure quality was being minted frequently tells us that the economy was stable and the rulers powerful.

It is difficult to say if the coins found in a hoard are typical of those in circulation at the time the hoard was collected. Sometimes this may be so, and the coins will match the pattern of coins built up from isolated finds. At other times, the hoard may contain mainly old or high value coins. This would suggest that it may have been one person's or a family's savings, built up over a number of years.

In many parts of the world people have managed without coins. They were unknown in the Aztec and Inca empires before the Spaniards arrived. In many parts of New Guinea they are still not used. This does not mean that these areas lacked currency, or special items which could be exchanged for a set number of articles. It is probable that in the European Stone Age, stone ax heads were used in this way. In Africa, copper ingots from the Congo area were widely traded in the period before European contact. In many areas useful items, such as ax or knife blades and fishhooks, became elaborated so that they were no longer of practical use. They served as tokens used only for the exchange of certain kinds of goods.

several ways. They can reveal links between the site where they were found and other places. The Sutton Hoo coins can all be shown to come from areas ruled by the Merovingian Franks (the earliest French kings) in the seventh century AD. Also coins can usually be dated and so indicate the earliest time at which they could have been deposited. Of course, we have to be careful with isolated finds. A Roman coin dug up in Ecuador does not prove the Romans reached South America! Coins can demonstrate long distance contacts as well. For example, many coins are copies of others. The gold *staters* of Phillip II of Macedon (who reigned from 359 to 336 BC) and his son Alexander the Great (who reigned from 336 to 323 BC over an empire stretching from Greece to India), were widely imitated by the Celts in northern Europe. The Celts gradually broke down the original designs and remade them into abstract patterns.

Weapons and War

People have always shown a remarkable willingness to destroy each other. There are countless remains of weapons and victims to prove it. Weapons first may have originated as hunting tools. Perhaps they were turned against other human beings over claims to property, food or land. By looking at the shape of weapons we can trace how they developed. Many different weapons grew from the simple chopper tools and handaxes of the Old Stone Age. By 10,000 BC there were many specialized weapons, such as flaked stone arrowheads, spears with stone or fire-hardened wood points, and bone harpoons.

Weapons are found in many sites, although usually only the inorganic parts are well preserved. Thus metal sword blades and stone projectile heads from spears and arrows are recovered, as are sling or catapult shot, or iron bolts fired from Roman or medieval siege engines. But the wooden sword grips, arrow shafts and catapult machinery have long since rotted in the soil. In later sites guns may be found, especially bronze, brass, and iron cannon and the shot they fired. Iron cannonballs are sometimes still embedded in the masonry against which they were used. The spread of firearms into new areas may be traced by other remains. Rectangular Norfolk flints, used in the locks of guns imported during

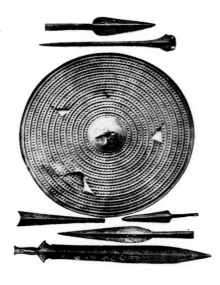

Bronze weapons found in the Thames River which date from 1000–500 BC. From top to bottom: Spearhead, rapier, parade shield, daggers, spearhead and sword. The handles and other non-metallic parts had of course long since rotted away.

Greek bronze statuette of a helmeted warrior on horseback, made about 550 BC.

The impressive hillfort of Maiden Castle was defended by British warriors against the invading Romans. Some of the slain were found buried near the intricate eastern gateway (top left).

Model of a Roman ballista of the type used in the assault on Maiden Castle.

the past few hundred years, are found all over West Africa, long after the guns themselves have disappeared. Some archaeologists have tried to test the efficiency of ancient weapons. For example, a model of a Roman ballista, a military engine for hurling stones and metal bolts, was made to test its range and speed of working. It proved extremely efficient!

It is impossible to say what proportion of the human race has been destroyed by warfare. But a few of the victims of war are sometimes discovered by archaeologists. The Iron Age fort of Maiden Castle in Dorset was stormed by the Roman army soon after it invaded Britain in 43 AD. Excavations inside the huge earthwork defenses revealed the skeletons of thirty-eight Britons buried hastily during the assault. They still wore bronze anklets and toe rings which showed that they were humble warriors and not great lords. The slashing cuts of swords,

stabs from legionaries' short swords, and small, square holes in skulls made by throwing spears revealed the devastating effect of Roman weapons. One man was found with the remains of a metal arrowhead still embedded in his spine. Nearby 20,000 slingshots were found, stacked ready for use against the invading forces.

The effects of weapons and warfare are reflected in a variety of ways. The introduction of the stirrup into Europe in the eighth century AD led to the development of cavalry which could fight against each other on horseback. This helped to alter the whole pattern of European military tactics and led to pitched battles on level ground.

New weapons led to new systems of defense and may have caused men to abandon the territory they already held. Groups of people found it necessary to build elaborate defenses, such as the massive stone walls encircling many medieval towns. They had to modify their style of building; castle architecture changed when cannon began to be used. Round towers replaced square ones, which could easily be demolished by firing at their corners. Sometimes the relation between weapons, warfare, and changes in architecture is more indirect. It was the absence of war, partly due to the increase in royal power, which led to the disappearance of the English fortified manor house in the sixteenth and seventeenth centuries.

Magic
and Religion

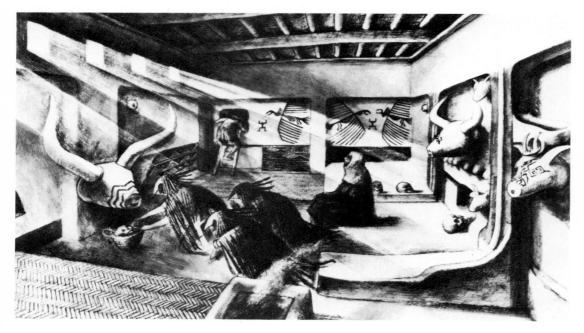

Reconstruction of a ceremony at Çatal Hüyük, about 6150 BC, based on wall paintings found there. The paintings show vultures with human legs placing human skulls in baskets on platforms below large bulls' heads. Finds at the site corroborate this evidence.

We do not know when religious beliefs and activities first began. Neanderthal people, 50,000 years ago, buried their dead in graves with flowers. This suggests some sort of belief that physical death was not a complete end. *Homo erectus* at Choukoutien, China, may have eaten human flesh, as fossilized bones suggest. Although we cannot be certain, scholars believe that it may have been part of a ceremony to appease the spirits of the dead, to gain the power of the dead person, or simply out of affection.

By the time that the first cities began to develop, evidence for religious beliefs becomes clearer. In Jericho, human skulls with features modeled in plaster and shell-inlaid eyes, made about 7000 BC, may show that the townspeople revered their ancestors. A shrine dating from about 6000 BC was found at Çatal Hüyük, Turkey, in which human skulls were placed near to large modeled bulls' heads.

Nearly all archaeological evidence about religion and ritual is difficult to interpret. We cannot easily or safely reconstruct what human beings believed in from material remains alone. When we excavate a ninth century Anglo-Saxon church or a Hindu temple, we can form some idea of the ceremonies performed in it and the beliefs behind them, because these are temples of religions and traditions which still exist. When we excavate great Maya ceremonial centers in Central America, however, we can do little more than guess at the details of the rituals once held there. But from the pictures of the gods carved on temple walls, we can tell that our ancestors worshiped forces that were vital to their lives, such as the sun, moon, rain, and the fertility of the land.

Many female figurines made of clay or stone are found in archaeological sites. Some archaeologists have taken them as evidence of a widespread cult of a "mother goddess," possibly associated with fertility. Others have suggested they may have had a variety of uses, perhaps as dolls or memorials to dead women. Maybe they were simply intended to show ideal feminine beauty. We will never know for certain what the owners believed about them.

Where written evidence exists the matter is far easier. As writing developed, professional priests emerged in many towns and cities. Their inscriptions in temples or on tablets may throw light on beliefs and practices. Therefore, we can learn a great deal from writings about the religions of Mesopotamia and ancient Egypt, the names of their gods and their special powers. Occasionally, archaeology may also show how writings of the time have not revealed all the religious beliefs. At Ur, in Sumer, graves were discovered dating from about 2500 BC. A queen called Shudu-Ad lay in one of these, elaborately ornamented. With her were her priests, soldiers, and a wagon pulled by asses, its drivers and all her ladies in waiting who had accompanied her into death. No one had suspected such burials from religious texts written at the time.

We can also gain an idea of beliefs from the offerings left at shrines. Sometimes they indicate that some particular kind of help was wanted. At the Roman temple at the source of the Seine River in France, models of parts of the human body were found. Worshipers left hands and feet made of clay showing rheumatism and little busts of people with goiter, eye infections, and symptoms of mental illness. They hoped the god of healing would cure them of these illnesses. Objects from the Roman temple at Lydney Park, Gloucester, England, have also been interpreted as showing man's belief in the god's concern with healing.

The Venus of Willendorf dates from 40,000 BC. Small female figurines like this were believed to bring fertility and success in hunting.

Assur was originally god of Ashur, the religious capital of Assyria. After 1800 BC he was regarded as the country's chief god.

One of the decorated human skulls found at Jericho. It dates from about 7000 BC.

Graves
and Tombs

Many peoples believe that after death the spirit lives on, even if only for a short time. When death occurs it is usually dealt with by a religious or magical ceremony. Part of this will be concerned with disposing of the body of the deceased. How the dead person is treated depends very much on his or her position while alive. The poor, the young, and the unimportant usually receive far less attention than the rich and powerful.

The human practice of disposing of the dead in a ceremonial way is of great use to archaeologists. Burials or cremations provide not only skeletal remains but often grave goods which relate to the lives of the individuals.

It is natural that the spectacular burials of the aristocracy should attract most popular attention. Probably the most famous of these is the tomb of Tutankhamun, a young Egyptian king of the fourteenth century BC, excavated in the 1920s. The tomb, which contained the mummified body of Tutankhamun himself, had largely escaped the attention of tomb robbers. It revealed the incredible wealth with which the Egyptians surrounded their pharaohs. There were chariots covered with gold and bronze, alabaster vases, and even containers filled with food, such as roast duck, for his afterlife. Almost as impressive are the tombs of the Bronze Age Chou dynasty in China dating from 1027 to 475 BC, in which, at the bottom of a pit, men were buried near chariots with the horses to pull them.

In many cultures, important burials are covered with large mounds or barrows. This indicates the amount of labor which could be organized and channeled into commemorating the society's leaders. The Hopewell people of the American Midwest are particularly famous for the huge burial mounds which they built for their chiefs. The size of these monuments indicates that, although these people were hunters and gatherers, they were neverthe-

The dry sand of the Atacama Desert, Chile, has preserved the hair and skin of this body for hundreds of years.

less a settled and prosperous society and could devote much time and labor to activities other than basic subsistence.

Humbler burials can also provide a great deal of information. Cremations are also informative. The remains are usually placed in special containers which often indicate the dead person's homeland. Scientific examination of the skeletons can indicate the ages at which people died or were killed, how many men and women in a group, and the diseases from which they suffered. Grave goods can indicate

Tattoo of a deer with an eagle's beak and long antlers, found on the right arm of the chief buried in a barrow at Pazyryk, USSR.

their trading links and the kind of jewelry and clothes they would have owned when they were alive.

In some parts of the world, the weather conditions under which corpses are disposed of helps preserve the flesh of the bodies. The dry, desert climate of parts of coastal Peru leads to a natural mummification of bodies, leaving skin and hair almost intact. The burials at Pazyryk in the Altai Mountains, Siberia, were preserved by intense cold which helped prevent bacteria destroying the remains. Many leather, cloth, and wooden items were found in a remarkable state of preservation after 2500 years. Large pieces of human skin, some of it elaborately tattooed, were also recovered.

A single group of people may dispose of its dead in several different ways. In West Africa today, for example, priests may be interred under the floors of their homes. The bones of kings are kept in special mausolea. Ordinary people are buried in coffins in areas of a village cemetery reserved for their clan or family. In the past slaves were buried without coffins away from the main cemetery, and young children and convicted criminals tumbled into very shallow graves in the village rubbish dump!

Howard Carter, the British archaeologist, and Lord Carnarvon discovered the tomb of the ancient Egyptian Pharaoh Tutankhamun in 1922. This jumble of furniture, including the splendid cow-bed in the center, is the first view that Carter and Carnarvon had of what proved to be a very important and exciting archaeological discovery.

Home Life

Did Stone Age mothers sing lullabies to their children? We shall never know. But we may get a good idea of where they sat while they nursed them by examining the things they dropped on the floor of their living areas. A pattern can be worked out from finds, such as spindle whorls and needles, or broken tools, which shows what went on in different parts of the home. This often indicates if areas were usually occupied by women or men. Excavations of a hunter's camp in northern France showed how, at about 10,000 BC, flint knapping (chipping) was done near the fireplace. From the way the waste flakes of stone lay it was possible to tell that the flint worker always sat with his or her back or side to the fire. Other excavations have shown definite areas for sleeping and preparing food.

At Mesa Verde in Colorado many small villages have been found tucked away in large natural caves in the canyon walls. These settlements were built by the Anasazi Indians during the period 900–1300 AD, and were carefully planned to use all the shady, defensible space. Houses were arranged in family groups of eight to fifteen rooms around courtyards. Each group had a kiva or circular ceremonial subterranean room used only by men. Some multi-storied apartment-like buildings were constructed as well as tall lookout towers, water storage cisterns and canals. The inhabitants ate turkey, cottontail, rock squirrel and deer, and used wooden digging sticks in the cultivation of corn, beans and squash. Many remains of basketwork, matting and clothing have been found such as sandals of twilled yucca and warm, feathered socks for winter wear.

Humans have lived in a vast variety of houses and shelters, ranging from the small domed mud-brick houses of the early Neolithic people of Cyprus to the

The site at Skara Brae in the Orkney Islands, where a complete Neolithic village was discovered after a violent storm blew away the sand dune which had covered it for 4000 years. Because wood was scarce in the area, the villagers had used stone to build and furnish their houses, which is why everything is so well preserved. The photograph shows how cupboards, shelves and box beds were made of stone slabs and set into the drystone walls.

Archaeologists have been able to reconstruct many types of ancient dwellings. The hut shown far left was made from mammoth bones, poles and hide in the Ukraine, about 30,000 years ago. The houses shown center and right are from Pan P'o, a Neolithic village dated 4000 BC, in Shensi Province, China.

wooden longhouses of the Vikings. All buildings, where enough evidence survives, show a deliberate arrangement of rooms or living areas. This suggests that the people living there felt that particular places were right for particular tasks. Archaeologists have excavated groups of simple Maya one-roomed houses built on raised mounds around the edge of a plaza. The houses show that some were used for cooking, some for sleeping, and others, usually the grandest or biggest, were small shrines with decorated walls where the gods of rain or the moon may have been worshiped.

In many dwellings the fire, the center of domestic life and food preparation, seems to have been the most important area of the home from which everything else radiated. Even where there are no walls, for example in a hunter's camp, fires mark out divisions within a large group. Among modern Bushmen of the Kalahari Desert, even the most temporary camp is given a basic division by erecting simple marker posts. Each fire forms the center of separate families or kin groups, and a person may not walk casually from one fire to another. The same rule may well have applied to Stone Age hunters and gatherers.

In early societies, most things needed by the family were made at home, rather than bartered or bought from specialist craftsmen. Clothes, cooking utensils, and tools were among the most important things produced. Usually men were the toolmakers, but men or women may have made pottery, prepared skins, or woven cloth. Often archaeologists can only guess at the clothes prehistoric people wore. The cloth and skin have usually rotted away, leaving only the fastenings. Most clothes were simple wrap-around garments held in place with ties, belts, brooches, or pins. Remains of spindle whorls, loom weights and bone weaving combs and needles give clues to weaving techniques. Special stone tools, such as scrapers, and bone needles, are evidence that skin and fur were prepared and used for clothing and bedding.

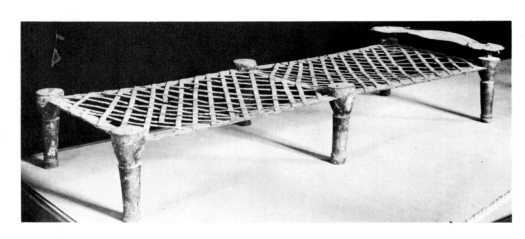

A bronze bed made by the Etruscans, about 350 BC.

Models, Toys and Games

Many doll-like figurines and models of animals, houses, furniture, and vehicles have been found in archaeological excavations. To us they look like toys, but to the people who made them they had a very different meaning. Most of these finds come from the graves of adults, not children, and there is the major clue. These miniature objects were put into the grave or tomb as grave goods, which the dead person would be able to use in the afterlife.

Sometimes important people, such as Tutankhamun of Egypt, Queen Shudu-Ad of Sumer, and Chinese princes and princesses, were buried with all their jewels, household goods, and sometimes their servants. Less important people had to make do with models of these things. At about 3000 BC pottery models of log houses were made in central Europe. Many clay models of four-wheeled carts have been found in graves in Transylvania, in the northwest of modern Rumania.

Some real toys, however, have survived to the present day. The dry sands of Egypt have preserved roughly made rag dolls, wooden animals on wheels, and stone mice with moveable jaws and tails. One of the oldest and most complicated toys, made in Egypt at about 1900 BC, is a set of small ivory dwarfs fitted onto a box. The dwarfs were made to dance by pulling strings. The ancient Greeks and Romans also made toys for their children. At about 400 BC they played with jointed wooden and clay dolls. A very cleverly designed clay doll was made, which mimicked the actions of a woman rolling out pastry with a rolling pin. Roman children played with lead soldiers just as modern children do. Paintings on vases show Greek children playing with balls, tops, and whips, over 2000 years ago

Games were as popular then as now. One of the most popular games of the classical world was knucklebones. The pieces were originally small bones from the ankle joints of cloven-footed animals,

Girl on a swing: an ingenious toy made about 1500 BC on the island of Crete.

such as sheep and goats, but many copies were made in ivory, wood or stone. The game was to throw the knucklebones up into the air and try to catch them on the back of the hand. Knucklebones were also used as dice, though the modern kind of six-sided dice was also known to the Greeks and Romans. Each knucklebone had four differently molded sides, each of which had a different value. Four knucklebones were thrown at a time and the scores added. Many combinations of values had nicknames such as "Old Woman" and "Aphrodite." Counters were used with knucklebones to play a kind of backgammon. Some counters had inscriptions on them saying MALE(E)ST (bad luck) or VICTOR (winner)

Several gaming boards have survived for 5000 years. Unfortunately, the rules have not. Five gaming boards of about 3000 BC were found in the royal graves at Ur. The most beautiful of these is completely covered with shell plaques inlaid with brilliant blue lapis lazuli and red limestone. The board is hollow and contained the counters and dice. There are seven white and seven black counters and three white and three blue pyramid-shaped dice. The ancient Egyptians played a game called Senet on a very similar board. Like the Sumerian game, the board is hollow and contained the pieces, but it also has another game marked out on the reverse side. For the second game, the board was marked with three columns of ten squares. Two sets of ten men were used; one set was spool-shaped, the other conical. Both Senet and the Game of Thirty Squares were very important to the ancient Egyptians, who believed that the spirits of the dead played these games in the afterlife.

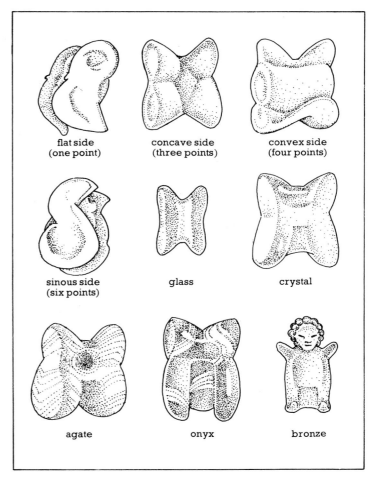

Knucklebones were sometimes used as dice. Special knucklebones were made from semi-precious stones, bronze, or glass.

One of the gaming boards found at Ur, with round counters and dice.

Recreating the Past

All archaeology is an attempt to reconstruct part of the past. The archaeologist takes the information and objects he recovers from the earth, and uses his skills and imagination to bring them to life. Making models or drawing pictures can show us vanished worlds. They can also suggest new lines of inquiry to the archaeologist, who may not have considered certain points of construction or detail.

The best archaeological artists are those who have a firm understanding of the sites they illustrate. They show how ruined houses, castles, and temples might

have looked where people once lived, worked, fought and worshiped. People are always included in reconstruction drawings to give us an idea of the scale of the buildings. The scene is drawn from a bird's eye view to give an idea of the whole site.

Carefully built scale models help to change a complicated archaeological site into a three-dimensional form which can be easily understood. But sometimes full-scale, real life re-enactments are made. On Easter Island, isolated in the South Pacific Ocean, the famous voyager Thor Heyerdahl led an investigation into how the island's huge stone figures were quarried, moved several miles to their final site, and then erected on stone platforms. Using the advice and labor of native Easter Islanders and having studied unfinished statues in the quarries, he completed one figure by using old stone picks to chip away the rock.

One hundred and eighty Easter Islanders dragged the statue to its site. Twelve men with poles levered the statue, while another man slipped pebbles and larger stones underneath to build up a wedge-shaped ramp. After eighteen days of painstaking work the statue fell into its prepared base. From this reconstruction exercise, Heyerdahl was able to calculate the labor and time involved in such a

The Acropolis of Copán (right) reconstructed according to the work of Alfred Maudslay. The Ball Court (above) is 86 feet long and 23 feet wide with a slanting walk rising to two small temples. First built in about 250 AD it was then rebuilt in 514 AD and again in 775 AD. It is to the left of the main complex in the reconstruction drawing.

project. He drew conclusions about the original inhabitants and their society between 1000 and 1700 AD when the other statues were put in place. There must have been very powerful chiefs to organize the hundreds of stone carvers and laborers involved in producing and erecting all these great stone giants.

The city of Copán in Honduras was built by the Mayas during their greatest period 400–800 AD. In 1885 Alfred Maudslay began uncovering and mapping the huge ruined site which was later restored by the Carnegie Institution of Washington after extensive excavation. The Acropolis was the focal point of the city. It contained many temples, ceremonial staircases, inscribed stelae and altars.

Perhaps the most moving reconstructions are those of musical instruments. After hundreds or even thousands of years, we can hear once again the sounds which delighted long-dead priests and kings. The completely squashed remains of a shell-inlaid harp, with a wonderful bull's head in gold, its eyes, beard, and horntips of lapis lazuli, were found in the Sumerian royal graves at Ur. It has been put back together again with painstaking detective work. A stringed instrument from the Sutton Hoo ship burial has been remade in two different ways, as a harp and as a lyre. It has been played in public to accompany recitations of the great Anglo-Saxon poem *Beowulf*.

Sometimes reconstructions are on a grand scale. Ruined buildings and whole sites are cleared and rebuilt to show them at their finest time. The great Maya city of Tikal in Guatemala was carefully cleared of jungle which had invaded it and caused stelae (upright slabs) and masonry to fall. Many years of excavation work followed. An equally long time was spent on replacing stone blocks, reinforcing dangerous walls and recreating the architecture of the enormous pyramid temples.

The most elaborate reconstructions are those which depend upon repopulating the rebuilt sites with living people and animals. In 1977 a group of English people volunteered to live in Iron Age conditions, with virtually no contact with the modern world, for a whole year. They survived, with only a few drop-outs, but none would care to repeat the experiment!

The completed reconstruction of the smaller harp.

Two crushed harps dating from 2750 BC, revealed during the excavation of the Death Pit at Ur.

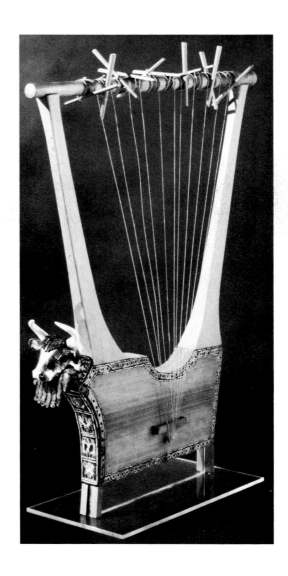

The Story in Pictures

In the nineteenth century, the great cave paintings of the Old Stone Age were rediscovered at places such as Les Eyzies in France and Altamira in Spain. They had been preserved almost perfectly underground for 20,000 years or more. Everyone was surprised and puzzled, for here was a sophisticated art which seemed to date back to man's earlier days. We still do not know how art began. There are many theories about the cave paintings and especially about the animals many of them depict, the bison, horses, mammoths, and reindeer. Perhaps they were painted for the joy of self-expression and no more. Were they magical to ensure success in hunting? Some pictures show wounded animals and what seem to be spear or arrow marks. Perhaps the paintings were intended to encourage animals to breed and multiply. Or perhaps they were simply signs of the hunters' knowledge. Maybe their makers revered them as totems, or symbols, of their tribe. No one is sure of the truth, for we cannot test these theories.

Recently, archaeologists have examined how frequently certain types of painting, such as horses, bison, and of various abstract signs – wavy lines and geometric shapes – occur in caves. They have pointed out how certain animals and abstract signs are grouped together in various wall paintings.

The fact that artists create images does not mean that those images can automatically be understood by people today. To interpret pictures or sculptures, the archaeologist must try to judge what the image meant to its makers, its relationship to other works of art, and its age. By studying where an image was used it is possible to get some broad idea of its purpose. Pictures on funerary pots or in tombs may have a special meaning. They may seem to show scenes of everyday life, but really depict stories of the gods. But what is the meaning of the Folkton Drums? These are three chalk cylinders found in a child's grave in north Yorkshire and carved with highly stylized

The Mimbres potters of New Mexico, 1000–1200 AD, made pots such as this for use as grave goods.

faces. There are many mysteries like this that we shall probably never understand.

Some pictures tell us a little more. The great stone friezes from Assyria, carved about 650 BC, show scenes of lion hunting, battles and ceremonial processions. They illuminate a part of that society's life even though they show only the nobility and not the ordinary people. The pictures on Maya temples,

Two views of one of the Folkton Drums, found in Yorkshire, England. It is a piece of carved chalk which dates from the early part of the Bronze Age.

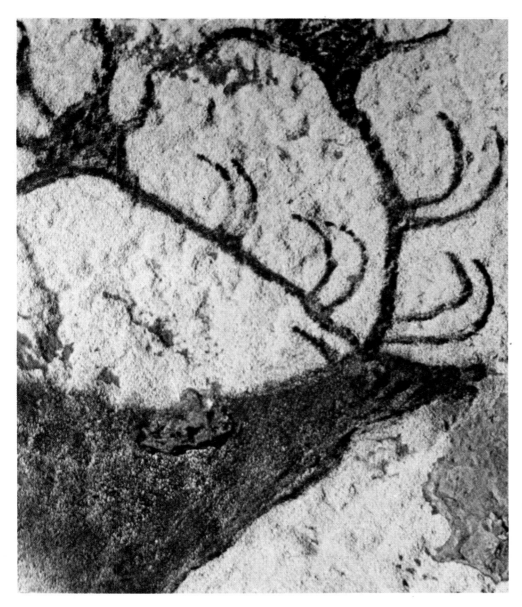

Painting of a stag with exaggerated antlers dating from the Old Stone Age. It is in the caves of Lascaux in the Dordogne valley in France. This cave system, discovered in 1940 contains some of the finest known prehistoric cave paintings.

painted pots and stelae can also be interpreted. They portray grand processions and sacrifices. The paintings on the pots of the Moche people of Peru show many everyday scenes such as fishing or hunting, although the clothes some figures wear suggest that the scenes really illustrate myths about the gods.

In dealing with pictures archaeologists have to be cautious. They must consider the circumstances in which they were found and compare them with others from similar sites. Above all they must never try to force a meaning on them. Archaeologists, unlike cultural anthropologists, cannot talk to the people they study. Their information always comes from the past to the present. Archaeologists must accept that they may never be able to understand with certainty some of the messages.

Treasure Hunters

Throughout the ages people have dreamed of finding buried treasure. Almost always the riches are imagined as the great funeral treasure of long-departed kings or rulers who were interred with all the wealth that they had displayed in life. There have probably been tomb robbers for as long as there has been the tradition of putting goods in graves. When Howard Carter was in the early stages of excavating the tomb of Pharaoh Tutankhamun he was disturbed to see that the doors had been opened and resealed. This indicated that tomb robbers might have been at work there soon after the death of Tutankhamun in 1352 BC as the seals were those of the ancient Egyptian custodians. It was evident from the disarray of objects in the ante room to the burial chamber itself that robbers had indeed entered, but had been interrupted by officials. Lids were askew on jars and boxes which contained precious oils and perfumes, and there were skin containers nearby in which the liquids were to be carried away. On the floor lay a small linen bundle which contained several heavy gold rings grabbed by the thieves but perhaps dropped during their arrest. The custodians had stacked up the ransacked boxes and pieces of furniture, resealed the doors and left their god-king to rest peacefully. Clearly the lust for treasure was so strong even then that people were prepared to run the risk of dreadful curses put on the tombs of the Pharaohs in order to loot the fabulous riches which they contained.

Tomb robbing has also been carried out for pseudo-scientific reasons. Between 1815 and 1819, Giovanni Belzoni, a giant ex-circus strongman, smashed his way into Egyptian tombs. He removed the more striking or saleable objects, including some remarkable mummies, and abandoned or destroyed the rest. Heinrich Schliemann, who rediscovered the ancient city of Troy, smuggled out some of his most precious finds under his wife's skirt!

Toward the end of the last century, archaeologists began to turn their attention away from hunting for treasures. They started to concentrate on increasing their knowledge of the past, recovering everything they could from the earth and carefully recording and publishing their findings. Then other scholars could study and, if necessary, correct their interpretations.

Unfortunately, as archaeology has developed and become more widely publicized, many people wish to own archaeological pieces simply because they are rare or beautiful and their possession brings pleasure. Today this desire keeps treasure hunters, grave robbers, and fakers in business.

Sophia Schliemann wearing the so-called jewels of Helen found during her husband's dig at Troy in 1873.

Belzoni removed massive sculptures from ancient Egyptian sites, as well as taking many smaller treasures.

Crowds gathered to watch Heinrich Schliemann's excavation of the royal graves at Mycenae, Greece.

Tomb-robbing continues to be a problem. In Colombia much valuable archaeological evidence has been lost because of robbers.

In many parts of Latin America professional looters, called *guaqueros*, are highly skilled at detecting ancient burial sites from which they remove gold-work, pottery, and cloth. The sites are dug quickly and crudely, and much valuable evidence is destroyed forever. Some looters are highly organized and violent. Planes and helicopters have been used to fly out pieces of carved stone sliced off Maya stelae hidden in the jungle. Many crucial inscriptions have been defaced or destroyed. Some of those who have tried to prevent this have been murdered. The problem is almost worldwide. In Ghana, funerary sites rich in terra-cotta human heads representing ancestors were secretly located and stripped. In Italy, Etruscan tombs have been robbed of their contents and their murals.

Modern archaeologists loathe treasure hunting. It destroys evidence and thrives on people's greed. Many countries have passed laws to stop unofficial excavations and also to stop items illegally obtained from being taken from one country to another. However, the problem continues, and metal detectors have recently made the problem worse. Amateur treasure hunters, encouraged by stories of finds of coins or precious metals, dig where they will and often keep or sell anything they find. It is very important for us to realize the harm done by such illegal activity. We must treasure what should be everyone's to see and enjoy.

Gold and Goldsmiths

The gleam of gold has always fascinated mankind. It was probably the first metal to be discovered and used because in some forms it is both easy to see and to obtain. It occurs in nuggets, in river sands and in veins in quartz. Early man would have found it very simple to collect nuggets or pan river beds.

By about 4000 BC the people of Mesopotamia had discovered one of the curious properties of gold. Unlike other metals, it does not become brittle and crack when it is hammered, but can be beaten into thin sheets. In Peru, a goldsmith's grave dated to about 2000 BC shows us that there, too, gold nuggets were being hammered flat. The earliest ornaments were made by cutting gold sheet to shape and by decorating it with shallow engravings. Sometimes designs were hammered out from the back of the

sheet to make slightly raised, *repoussé*, ornaments. Bowls, helmets, and cups were made by beating gold sheet over shaped wooden, stone, or resin molds or templates.

In the ancient world gold was used mainly for making personal ornaments. It was also used for making special ceremonial objects, such as precious cups, scepters, and masks to be put over the faces of dead kings or chiefs. The Indians from Mexico to Ecuador used gold for making such everyday objects as fish-hooks, needles, and tweezers. From about 600 BC gold, silver, and a naturally occurring alloy of the two, electrum, were used to make the world's first coins. These circulated in the Mediterranean area and were used in the wine and olive oil trade.

Gold is often found as a pure metal. Therefore, unlike copper and iron, it need not be subjected to complicated smelting processes. The nuggets or grains simply have to be melted at a temperature of 1975°F. This kind of heat could be produced by using a hollow cane as a blow pipe and blowing air by mouth onto glowing charcoal. Later, furnaces were built with bellows to provide the draft.

Not all the gold we see in museums is pure gold.

Gold torque, or neck-ring, from Snettisham, Norfolk, England, made about 100 BC.

A collection of gold objects including a helmet, face-mask and jewelry made of gold and copper alloy found in Colombia.

Gold and lapis lazuli jewelry from the Death Pit at Ur, Sumer, about 2750 BC.

It was soon discovered that a mixture of 80 per cent gold to 20 per cent copper produced an alloy with all the color and quality of gold, but with a much lower melting point. This made the casting of gold ornaments much easier. Rounded, three-dimensional gold objects could be made using molds and then decorated using other goldworking techniques such as filigree and granulation. In filigree work, gold strips were made into gold wire by drawing them through different shaped perforations. The wires were then bent into shape on the back plate, formed into borders, spirals, and curves, and soldered into place. For granulation, small spherical drops of gold, or granules, could be made by dropping molten gold into cold water, where it solidified. The tiny granules were also soldered into position. It is amazing how delicate the work is when you consider that ancient goldsmiths had no electricity or magnifying glasses to help them.

Many peoples in different parts of the world have used the lost-wax method, or *cire perdue*, for casting complicated gold ornaments. The Sumerians used this ingenious technique as early as 2800 BC. The ancient goldsmiths of Colombia and Ecuador were producing charm-like animal pendants in this way by about 500 BC.

The object desired in gold was first modeled in beeswax over a clay core. It was then decorated with coils of fine wax threads and details such as eyes and hair were added. The wax model was in turn covered with clay, which was allowed to harden. When hard, the whole thing was heated, the wax melted and poured out through specially made tubes leaving a hole in the clay coating. Next, the molten gold was poured into the empty space and allowed to solidify and cool. Then the clay mold was broken to reveal the golden object inside. Finally, it would be cleaned and polished using fine sand, smooth pebbles, and bone tools.

The stages of lost-wax casting (below) which the craftsman who made the frog (right) used.

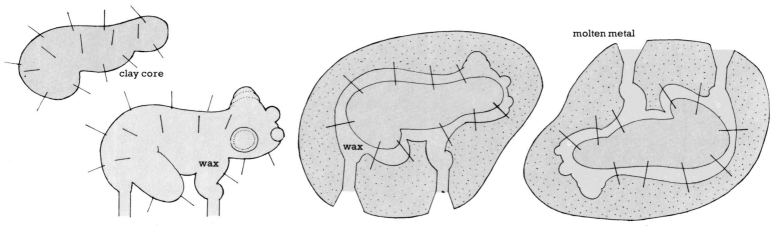

clay core

wax

wax

molten metal

Myths, Legends and Reality

To help them understand their own ancient histories many societies have developed myths and legends. Archaeologists continually strive to break through these myths and grasp the past as it really was. Occasionally, they find that a few of these myths contain cores of truth.

Perhaps the most appealing and widespread myths are those which recount the existence of a former golden age. One such myth is that of Atlantis. It was mentioned by the Greek philosopher Plato as a great civilization, which was swept beneath the sea by the gods because of the wickedness of its people. The story of the vanished glories of Atlantis has been used by people who prefer to believe extraordinary reasons for what happens in the world. They have regarded Atlantis as the origin of ancient American civilizations, of flying saucers and of the islanders of the Pacific Ocean. However, some archaeologists

have begun to suggest Plato's tale may contain a grain of truth. In the fifteenth century BC, the island of Thera, 75 miles north of Crete, was destroyed by a vast volcanic explosion. There is evidence that the great Minoan civilization of Crete disintegrated at about the same time. It has been suggested that the destruction at the Minoan palace of Knossos was the result of volcanic ash and gases. So Plato's story of Atlantis may express a dim memory of the fall of Cretan civilization.

One of the most famous myths is that of El Dorado. The first Europeans to reach South America heard tales of the vast golden wealth of one of its rulers. Moving inland, they found many peoples using gold, but never discovered the legendary golden ruler or his capital. By the mid-sixteenth century the myth of El Dorado had taken shape. He was a ruler who each year covered himself with gold dust, and in a great

A falling figure decked in ceremonial feathers and jade decorates this richly carved slab which covers the tomb of the Maya ruler, King Pacán, at Palenque, Mexico. This is the so-called astronaut tomb.

Lake Guatavita, Colombia, scene of the El Dorado ritual. The channel in the far shore was cut in one of the first attempts to drain away the water, in order to find the treasure. Below left is a gold model of the raft from which offerings were thrown into Lake Guatavita, during the El Dorado ceremony, between about 1000 and 1500 AD.

ritual threw many offerings of gold and emeralds into a sacred lake. People searched for this wealth mainly in Lake Guatavita in Colombia. From 1545 onward many attempts were made to drain it and recover the supposedly vast treasure it contains. Some gold was found, enough to convince and encourage later treasure hunters. In 1962 the Colombian authorities prohibited further attempts. The lake seems likely to keep its secrets. The truth about the riches of El Dorado will probably remain unknown.

Legends such as these often develop in the borderland between oral tradition and written his-

tory. Stories are passed down from one storyteller to another and the facts become hazy. Such is the legend of King Arthur. After the Romans had withdrawn from Britain in the fifth century AD, Anglo-Saxon invaders arrived. Some Britons, such as Arthur, returned to the hillforts of their ancestors and held out against them. There is little early written evidence about him, and some historians have dismissed him as a complete myth. Others have seen him as a British chieftain, possibly a cavalry leader. Recently, excavations have been carried out at the Iron Age hillfort of Cadbury Castle in Somerset, one of the sites traditionally associated with his capital, Camelot. They revealed that a timber hall with strong defenses had been built there in the fifth or sixth century AD. This points to the existence of an important local leader, which fits in with the general picture of the Arthurian legend. Perhaps, after all, Arthur is not a myth.

Archaeological remains and ruins often give rise to myths themselves, especially when there is apparently no simple explanation for them. Some authors have written about extraterrestrial influences and contacts revealed, for example, by the carving on a Maya tomb at Palenque, Mexico. Archaeologists have found no evidence whatsoever to support this theory.

Archaeology and Cultural Anthropology

Cultural anthropologists study living peoples, usually those who still live in small-scale, pre-industrial groups. They are interested in their customs, beliefs, social organization and technologies, and can observe these societies changing and developing. Unlike cultural anthropologists, archaeologists cannot watch the dead societies which they study, and we know that many important aspects of everyday life, such as the role of kinship and the basis of household organization, are lost to them. Even where remains such as temples, statues and paintings have survived, and clearly have a religious meaning, archaeologists working without documentary evidence can never be certain that their interpretation of the evidence from the soil is correct. Archaeologists, however, do not have to confine themselves to making purely factual statements about the technology and economy of the ancient peoples whom they study.

Information collected and analyzed by cultural anthropologists who have worked with present-day peoples living in similar environments and with tools and equipment similar to those studied by archaeologists can be of enormous help in interpreting archaeological evidence. Sometimes objects whose use has baffled the excavator can be identified and explained when they are compared with items in current use among so-called primitive peoples. Late Palaeolithic sites have produced small stone or bone hooks, or bone rods with a hook at one end. These might have remained mystery objects, but the hunting peoples of Australia, Africa and Latin America use precisely similar hooks as parts of their spear-throwers. It is a simple but very efficient piece of equipment which enables a hunter to increase the velocity and range of his spear. Such close similarities between archaeological and anthropological features are known as ethnographic parallels.

Less straightforward comparisons also can be made. For many years archaeologists thought that the life-style of ice-age hunters must have been extremely hard, dangerous and uncomfortable. How did these people manage to produce the marvels of Palaeolithic art when survival was ensured only by a ceaseless battle against nature? Research on the !Kung Bushmen of the Kalahari Desert and the Hadza of Tanzania has helped us to build a new picture of the daily life of Palaeolithic people. Both the Hadza and the !Kung are present-day hunters and gatherers who live in arid areas where there are few game animals. Studies by

Rock and cave paintings, left by the Bushman, or San, of South Africa and Lesotho, give us a vivid picture of the lives of hunter-gatherers.

In Mailu, Papua-New Guinea, women still make pots by building up and smoothing together coils of clay.

Men of the Pitjantjara group of Aborigines in their traditional hunting grounds near Alice Springs, central Australia.

cultural anthropologists have shown that their economies are remarkably sophisticated. Every possible resource of useful or edible material is exploited using an intimate knowledge of the ecosystem and seasonality of their territories. Although they live in impoverished environments these hunters and gatherers have considerable leisure time. Considering this point, it is far easier to imagine how Palaeolithic people, living when vast herds of animals roamed the plains and when the human population of the world was so small, managed to achieve so much.

One of the most important lessons which archaeologists have learned from their colleagues in cultural anthropology is that so-called primitive societies with very simple technologies are not necessarily crude in their spiritual beliefs and concepts. The Australian Aborigines had a wonderfully complex spiritual world and highly developed mythologies, oral histories, clan totems and sacred places. Superficially, though, the Aborigines appeared to have progressed very little along the road of technological achievement as they had only the simplest of tools and weapons.

We cannot, however, simply lift the details of such a well-known modern group and impose them willy-nilly on, for example, the mammoth hunters of the last ice age. Such anthropological information may indeed provide hints and guidelines which are an invaluable help to the archaeologist in fleshing out the bones of the past. But the danger of thinking of "primitive" peoples just as a kind of living archaeology must be avoided. They too have changed and developed over millennia and more recently have been molded and often undermined by contact with industrialized or western peoples.

Archaeology Tomorrow

Every day fresh archaeological discoveries are made. Road building schemes, industrial developments, agricultural expansion and observations from the air reveal previously unknown sites which may contain the keys to the secrets of past societies and civilizations. Unless such discoveries, whether they consist of a handful of unusual potsherds, a burial mound, or a complete settlement, can be monitored by archaeologists, irreplaceable evidence will be destroyed forever. It will be lost from the cultural heritage of the whole world. Desirable objects such as jewelry, carved stones or painted pottery vessels are often looted from unreported sites and sold for large sums of money to unscrupulous or unsuspicious private collectors. The trade in antiquities is now big business. National governments and international organizations such as UNESCO are campaigning to impose and enforce strict laws to protect our archaeological heritage. Even so a problem remains: how can we train, equip and finance the numbers of skilled archaeologists, conservators and scientists needed to cope with the modern crisis in the subject?

Universities are training increasing numbers of archaeologists who may obtain professional posts in museums, national parks, city or state governments or in university departments. There is still, however, a very important place in the world of archaeology for the amateur or part-time student. Local people have detailed knowledge of landscape, soils, drainage and land use and are often the first to spot unusual features which lead them to archaeological sites. Sometimes, with the help of local experts, they become involved in following up their discoveries and soon become deeply involved with the subject. Public enthusiasm for archaeology has become very great, possibly because of the contributions which individuals can make and because of the excitement of excavation. Responsible helpers are welcomed on excavations, and less energetic enthusiasts can lend a hand with the post-excavation work of processing the finds; washing, sorting, drawing and listing all the material vital to the understandng of the site. Many museums need similar help in organizing and cataloging their collections. Evening classes, summer schools and popular magazines are available to help the amateur learn about the subject.

The increase in public interest in archaeology has coincided not only with a boom in the rate of archaeological discoveries but also with a revolution in archaeological thinking. Scientific techniques which only became available in the late 1960s have transformed the subject into what is often called the New Archaeology. In this approach the archaeologist aims for the total reconstruction of the prehistoric society which he or she may be studying. Two of the most important elements in the New Archaeology are the use of computers for rapid and complex analysis of archaeological information and the growing reliance on absolute dating methods. More precise dates will soon be produced by a new way of measuring radiocarbon which is being developed even now. A great advantage of this method is that it uses only a few milligrams of sample material and is also much speedier than the older techniques.

The New Archaeology is particularly concerned with the interaction between humans and their environment, the ecosystem and the economic basis of prehistoric society. Obvious features such as temple complexes are no longer the exclusive subjects of excavation and research. Instead the whole surrounding area is considered, systematically surveyed and the function of the temple in the settlement pattern of the society analyzed. To complete the total reconstruction more use is made of anthropological data and speculative reconstructions of religious and social life have been attempted.

Ancient societies may soon be even more dramatically brought to life when their as-yet-indecipherable writings have been decoded. Perhaps when the script carved on wooden boards by the Easter Islanders can be read we shall discover fascinating details about why and when they erected the enormous stone statues. Work continues on translating Maya hieroglyphs; we now have names of rulers, cities and gods, planets, and stars. One day we may be able to read the details of their history and mythology.

Thus archaeology continues to grow as a subject composed of a broad spectrum of different specialties.

This is a small part of one of the most amazing recent archaeological discoveries: the army of the Chinese emperor Ch'in Shih Huang-Ti who died in 200 BC. He wanted to have his soldiers with him in the afterlife, but instead of having them killed and buried with him as earlier emperors had done, he had life-sized terra-cotta statues made. Two thousand years later archaeologists found them as they had been buried – in battle formation near their emperor's grave.

Everyone works together to understand how we humans have been shaped from the time of the australopithecines more than 3 million years ago.

Glossary

Absolute dating: new scientific dating methods help archaeologists give their finds precise dates, fixed in actual years. The principal laboratory dating methods are radiocarbon, potassium-argon, and thermoluminescence tests

Anatolia: the area which is now called Turkey

Artifact: any object made by human beings

Assyria: an ancient state of Mesopotamia (modern Iraq), which flourished from 1900 to 612 BC

Australopithecus: (means "Southern ape") the earliest known form of the human type, who lived at least three million years ago

Barrow: a mound of earth and stones raised over a burial

Chalcolithic: (means "copper and stone") the time when some objects were made of copper, but almost all tools were still made of stone

Classical: refers to the civilizations of ancient Greece and Rome (600 BC to 400 AD, their gods, art styles, and literature, which formed the basis of education and learning in the West until the present century

Cuneiform: the type of wedge-shaped writing on clay invented in Mesopotamia and used from about 3500 BC to 75 AD

Dendrochronology: ("tree-dating") the science of dating wooden objects by identifying patterns in the annual growth ring of the tree from which the artifact was made

Earthwork: an artificial bank of earth and stone, usually for defensive or ceremonial purposes

Eolith: (means "dawn stone") once thought to be the earliest type of stone tool, but now proved to be the result of natural forces of erosion

Feature: used in archaeology to denote things such as walls, pits, postholes, and hearths that are found during excavation

Fossil: ancient animal or plant remains preserved in rocks; usually only the harder parts, such as bones and woody stems, are fossilized

Grave goods: the objects placed in graves and tombs which were intended to equip the dead person in the afterlife

Hieroglyphs: (means "sacred carvings") the picture writing of the ancient Egyptians, used from about 3100 BC to 400 AD

Hominid: (from Latin "homo," a man) a member of the family that includes our apelike ancestors and man

Homo erectus: "upright man" first found in Africa one and a half million years ago, then throughout Africa and in the far East and Europe

Homo habilis: "handy man," represents another stage in human evolution, and lived about two million to one and a half million years ago

Homo sapiens: "wise man," the latest stage in human evolution including Neanderthal and modern man

Iberia: the ancient name for the large peninsula that is now divided into Spain and Portugal

Ideogram: a written sign or symbol that represents an idea

Industrial Revolution: the transformation from agricultural to industrial economies from about 1750 AD in northwestern Europe and North America

Inorganic: any material that is not made from a substance which has lived. Stone, clay, and metals are the most common inorganic materials

Mesolithic: (means the "Middle Stone Age") the period following the last glacial period, which spanned the gap between the hunters and gatherers of the Old Stone Age and the agricultural communities of the New Stone Age

Mesopotamia: (means the "land between two rivers") the area between the Tigris and Euphrates rivers where some of the world's earliest cities developed; today part of Iraq

Mummy: the body of a dead person, preserved to keep it lifelike

Neanderthal man: a probable ancestor of modern man *(Homo sapiens sapiens)* who lived 80,000 to 30,000 years ago, and is now extinct

Neolithic: (means the "New Stone Age") the period when people developed farming but still used stone tools

Organic: anything made of substances which have once lived, such as wood, charcoal, and bone

Palaeolithic: (means the "Old Stone Age") the period covering most of mankind's existence on earth, from the time of the hominids *Homo habilis* to the end of the last glacial period at about 10,000 BC

Pictograms: the earliest form of writing, in which objects are represented by pictures

Postholes: marks in the soil that show where upright timber posts of buildings, onto which walls or roofs were fixed, were set or driven into holes in the ground. The layout of postholes can reveal the plan of a building, and the depth can indicate the height of the posts which they once held

Potassium-argon dating: a method of absolute dating, based on the principle of radioactive decay in volcanic rocks

Potsherd: a piece of broken pottery

Proton magnetometer: a machine for measuring small differences in the earth's magnetic field which reveal buried archaeological remains

Radiocarbon dating: one of the most important scientific methods of dating archaeological finds, based on the principle of the steady decay of radioactive carbon 14 in all organic matter

Ramapithecus: a hominid that lived from about sixteen million years ago to about eight million

years ago, and seems to fill the gap between apes and Australopithecus

Section: the vertical side of an excavated trench in which the strata or layers can be seen and studied

Seed machine: a large water tank in which sieved soil is placed and through which air bubbles are then forced, making any organic material, especially small seeds, husks, and dried leaves, float to the surface. The plant remains are dried out and studied in order to discover what plants were used by the ancient inhabitants of a site

Soil resistivity meter: a machine to measure differences in the water content of the soil, by passing an electrical current through it to detect, for example, buried pits and ditches, which retain more moisture than the surrounding soils

Stratification: the way in which rocks, soils, clays, etc., in the earth form layers, the most recent ones lying on top of the earlier ones. The stratification of ancient sites is often complicated since the layers are sometimes mixed up and patchy

Sumer: the southern most part of Mesopotamia where civilization first began at about 3500 BC

Thermoluminescence: (means "giving out light when heated") a scientific dating method based on the fact that when pottery is heated, it will give out light that can be measured. The more light that is given out, the older the object

Index

Abu Simbel 42–43
aerial photography 10–11, 92
Anatolia 53, 60, 62, 64, 66, 94
Anglo-Saxons 18–19, 21, 25, 34, 44, 68, 72, 81, 89
animals 36, 44–45, 50–51, 82
anthropology 90–91
antiquarians 6
art 81–82
Assyria 8, 56, 59, 73, 82, 94
Australopithecus 46–47, 94
Aztecs 7, 9, 69

barley 52–53, 54
Beaker people 21, 60–61
boats 66–67
bones 17, 19, 24–25, 36, 38, 46–47, 50–51, 53
bronze 21, 54, 64, 70
Bronze Age 7, 36, 45, 60, 62–63, 64, 70
burial mounds 6, 10, 14, 62–63, 75
burials 24–25
Calah 8
carbon 14, 26–27, 30, 95
Catal Hüyük 60, 72
cave paintings 81–82
Chalcolithic 60–61
chopper tools 48–49, 70
Choukoutien 50, 72
cities 54–55
civilization 8–9, 54–55
coins 6, 14, 17, 26, 36, 68–69
copper 21, 62, 86
Copper Age 60–61
cuneiform 8, 19, 56

dendrochronology 28–29, 94

earthworks 10, 45, 94
Easter Island 80, 91
economic archaeology 36–37
El Dorado 88–89
eoliths 48, 94
Etruscans 12, 13, 77
excavation 6, 12, 14–15, 16–17, 38, 39, 42, 44, 45, 54, 55, 92
experimental archaeology 44–45

fakes 32–33
farmers 44, 52–53, 60
fishing 36, 90–91
fluorine 25
fossils 6, 32, 46, 94
frauds 32–33

games 78–79
gathering 50–51
geology 6, 12
gods 72–73
gold 8, 9, 38, 60, 68, 86–87
graves 74–75
Greeks 6, 9, 27, 30, 39, 56–57, 63, 69, 78
Grimes Graves 37

half-life 26, 30
hand ax 46–47, 48–49, 70
Harappa 54–55
hieroglyphics 56–57, 94
historical archaeology 34–35
Hittites 64
home life 76–77
hominids 30, 46, 48, 50
Homo erectus 46, 49, 72, 94
Homo habilis 46–47, 48, 94
Homo sapiens 32, 94
Hopewell culture 61, 74
hunters, 36, 50–51, 52, 90–91

Iberia 60, 62, 64, 95
ideogram 56, 95
Incas 9, 69
India 34, 51
Indus civilization 54–55, 57
industrial archaeology 40–41
Industrial Revolution 40–41, 42,
Iron 54, 95
Iron Age 7, 15, 36, 45, 64–65, 81, 89

jade 20, 38
Jericho 72–73

Knossos 9, 57, 88
Kon Tiki 67

Lascaux 51, 83
legends 88–89
Linear A 57
Linear B 57

Machu Picchu 9
Maiden Castle 71
maize 15, 22–23, 53, 61
mankind, origins of 46–47
Maya 9, 20, 38, 45, 72, 77, 81, 83, 85, 89
Mesolithic 36, 50, 95
Mesopotamia 8, 34, 53, 54, 56, 58, 60, 62, 66, 73, 95
metallurgy 60, 64, 86–87
Moche 6, 7, 83
Mohenjo Daro 54–55
mummies 22, 74–75
Mycenae 9, 27, 63, 85
myths 88–89

Nazca 11, 58
Neanderthal man 47, 72, 95
Neolithic 52–53, 77, 95
Nineveh 8
Nok culture 33, 65

obsidian 21, 61
Old Copper Culture 60–61
Old Stone Age 49, 82
Olduvai Gorge 31, 46–47, 48

Palaeolithic 33, 95
Pazyryk 75

Peking Man 47, 50
pictograms 56, 95
picturesque 81–82
Piltdown Man 25, 32
plants 8, 11, 22–23, 26, 36, 50–51, 52–53
potassium argon 30–31, 48, 95
pottery 12, 17, 19, 20, 30, 36, 54, 58–59, 91
prospecting methods 12–13
proton magnetometer 12–13, 95

radiocarbon 25, 26–27, 29, 30, 32, 92, 95
Ramapithecus 46, 95
recreating the past 80–81
religion 72–73, 74
rescue archaeology 42–43
Romans 6, 13, 34, 63, 70–71, 73, 78, 89
Rosetta Stone 56–57

satellite photography 11
seed machine 17, 23, 95
Shanidar 47
Skara Brae 76
soil resitivity meter 12–13, 95
Star Carr 36–37, 50
Stone Age 7, 36
Stonehenge 27, 60
stone tools 6, 20, 32, 36, 44, 46–47, 48–49, 50, 60
stratification 6, 14–15, 95
Sumer 58, 78, 81, 86–87, 95
Sutton Hoo 18–19, 23, 68, 74, 81

Taurus Mountains 52–53
Tehuacán valley 36, 53
thermoluminescence 30–31, 32, 95
tin 21, 62
tombs 74–75
toys 78–79
transport 66–67
treasure hunters 84–85
tree-ring dating 28–29, 94
Trelleborg 74–75
Troy 9, 63, 84
Tutankhamun 74–75, 78

underwater archaeology 38–39
Únětice culture 62–63
Ur 59, 73, 78, 81

Vikings 32, 35, 39, 44
villages 52–53

war 70–71
weapons 21, 25, 45, 49, 62–63, 64, 70–71
Wessex culture 21, 63
wheat 52–53, 54
wheels 54, 58–59, 66
writing 8, 33, 54, 56–57, 72

Zagros Mountains 52–53, 58

Credits

The Publishers gratefully acknowledge permission to reproduce the following illustrations:
Aerofilms 71l; Ancient Monuments Laboratory: Crown Copyright 21, 24t, 25l; Arizona State Museum University of Arizona 27b; Hallam Ashley 37b; Aspect Picture Library 38; A-Z Botanical Collection 28; Iris Barry 89b; Barnaby's Picture Library 49, 64; Warwick Bray 58t; Trustees of the British Museum 18br, 23, 32, 39l, 47l, 48, 57l, 59, 65tr, 67, 70, 73r, 81, 82b, 86c, r; British Tourist Authority 41l; California Institute of Technology (for NASA) 10; Camelot Research Committee 13; Peter Clayton 18bl, 20, 52, 57r, 68t, 69, 73l, 79, 85bl; Bruce Coleman Ltd. 15l, 8; Colorific 43, 91l; Daily Telegraph Colour Library 55; Robert Estall Photographs 11t, 17r, 27t, c, 41r; Werner Forman Archive 44; C. von Fürer-Haimendorf 51b; Ashmolean Museum, Oxford 75l; Susan Griggs Agency Ltd. 85br, 86l, 87, 88, 89t; Gerald H. Grosso 19t, c; Robert Harding Picture Library 12, 62; John Hillelson Agency 93; Hans Hinz 51t; Alan Hutchison Library 65b; Illustrated London News 72; G. J. Irwin 91r; P. R. Jones/Laeotoli Research Project 47r; Melvin E. Kester after Tatiana Proskouriakoff 80b; Keystone Press Agency 16, 17, 19b, 74; Livingstone Museum, Zambia 68b; Mansell Collection 8, 35bl, 40, 63, 66b, 70l, 73c, 77, 78, 84, 85; Merseyside County Museum, Liverpool 3r; Metropolitan Museum of Art 37t; Museum of Antiquities, Newcastle-upon-Tyne 71r; Museum of London 14, 15tr; National Monuments Record Air Photograph: Crown Copyright 11b; National Museum, Copenhagen 45; Ohio Historical Society 61t; Peabody Museum, Harvard University 82t; Ann and Bury Peerless 34; Photoresources 75t; John Picton 33r; Pictorial Colour Slides 61b; Picturepoint Ltd. 83; Popperfoto 24b; Josephine Powell 54; John Reader 31; Royal Anthropological Institute of Great Britain and Ireland 25r; St. Louis Art Museum 6; Salisbury and South Wiltshire Museum 7b; Scottish Tourist Board 76; Chosuke Serisawa, Tokoku 58b; Roger Viollet 33l, 65tl; Wasavarvet/Sjöhoriska museet, Stockholm 39c, r; York Archaeological Trust 35t; Universitets Oldsaksamling, Oslo 35b; University of Arizona/Laboratory of Tree Ring Research 29.
Cover Photograph: Susan Griggs Agency Ltd.
Artwork by: Linda Broad 23, 25, 50, 62, 79, 87; Mark Causer 60; Michael Craig 46, 48, 53, 76–7; James Roper 22, 46, 56; Swanston & Associates 8, 20, 52, 55; Technical Art Services 26, 29, 30, 36, 55.

Bibliography

Before Civilization, Colin Renfrew, Knopf, 1973
The Cambridge Encyclopedia of Archaeology, Andrew Sherratt, Crown, 1980
Introduction to American Archaeology (2 volumes), Gordon R. Wiley, Prentice-Hall, 1968–71
A History of American Archaeology, G. R. Willey and Jeremy A. Sabloss, Freeman, 1980
Science in Archaeology, D. Brothwell and E. Higgs, Praeger, 1969
Technology in the Ancient World, Henry Hodges, T. Y. Crowell, 1970